The Fellowship

Roy Williams

methuen | drama

LONDON • NEW YORK • OXFORD • NEW DELHI • SYDNEY

METHUEN DRAMA
Bloomsbury Publishing Plc
50 Bedford Square, London, WC1B 3DP, UK
1385 Broadway, New York, NY 10018, USA
29 Earlsfort Terrace, Dublin 2, Ireland

BLOOMSBURY, METHUEN DRAMA and the Methuen
Drama logo are trademarks of Bloomsbury Publishing Plc

First published in Great Britain 2022

A catalogue record for this book is available from the British Library.

A catalog record for this book is available from the Library of Congress.

ISBN: PB: 978-1-3503-4841-7
ePDF: 978-1-3503-4842-4
eBook: 978-1-3503-4843-1

Series: Modern Plays

Typeset by Mark Heslington Ltd, Scarborough, North Yorkshire

To find out more about our authors and books visit
www.bloomsbury.com and sign up for our newsletters.

The Fellowship had its premiere on 17 June 2022 at Hampstead Theatre, London, with the following cast and creative team.

Simone	**Rosie Day**
Jermaine	**Ethan Hazzard**
Tony	**Trevor Laird**
Marcia	**Suzette Llewellyn**
Sylvia / PC Spencer	**Cherrelle Skeete**
Dawn	**Lucy Vandi**

Writer	Roy Williams
Director	Paulette Randall
Designer	Libby Watson
Lighting	Mark Jonathan
Sound	Delroy Murray
Casting	Briony Barnett CDG
Associate Director	Grace Joseph
Assistant Designer	Roma Farnell

The Fellowship

For my beautiful mother, Gloria Rosene Kiffin Williams
Sunrise 1928 – Sunset 2019
I am here because you were there
X

'Every human being is an unprecedented miracle'
James Baldwin

Cast

Jermaine, *black, late teens*
Dawn, *black, early 50s*
Marcia, *black, mid 50s*
Tony, *black, early 50s*
Simone, *white, late teens*
PC Spencer, *black, late 20s*
Sylvia, *black, mid 20s*

The roles of **Sylvia** *and* **PC Spencer** *can be played by the same actor.*

Setting: A living room. A park bench.

Time: Autumn 2019.

Act One

Scene One

The living room

Jermaine *is wanting to leave.*

Jermaine It's no one you know, Mum.

Dawn Does this *no one* have a name?

Jermaine Course she has a name.

Dawn Which is?

Jermaine Say?

Dawn Her name boy, the girl must have a name.

Marcia You know she is not going to stop, Jermaine.

Jermaine Lume.

Dawn *Lume?*

Jermaine Yes, *Lume!*

Dawn Wat dat?

Jermaine Her name, Mum.

Dawn What kind of a name? Where is it from?

Jermaine (*a little thrown*) It's . . .

Marcia (*helping*) It's a Hindi name, right?

Jermaine Yes, of course. Hindi.

Marcia So she's Indian?

Jermaine Yeah, I mean no. I mean yes. Her parents are but she was born here. In England.

Dawn Right. And she is in your year?

Jermaine Yes.

Dawn   Same course as you?

Jermaine   Yes Mum, can I go now?

Dawn   Why do I have the feeling you are making this up?

Jermaine   I can't help with you that. May I please go?

Dawn   Marcia?

Marcia   What do you need, sis?

Dawn   Help me out please, with your lying through his no good teeth nephew.

Marcia   All rise!

Jermaine   You can't say all rise, Auntie, you are not a judge.

Marcia   Hush up. Raise your right hand. Do you swear by almighty God . . .

Jermaine   No, just cut to it please?

Marcia   Alright. Jermaine Patrick Adams, you are the son of Dawn Gloria Adams and Antony Edgar Collins, are you not?

Jermaine (*sighs*)   I am.

Marcia   And did Miss Dawn Adams issue you any instructions regarding your current relationship with a young woman who is yet to be identified?

Jermaine   I told you her name.

Marcia   Please answer the question, Mister Adams?

Jermaine   Lume!

Marcia   Otherwise you may find yourself in contempt of court.

Jermaine   I thought the judge says that?

Marcia   Mister Adams?

Jermaine   Yes, she did.

Marcia   And Mister Adams, do you usually follow your mother's instructions?

Jermaine   Objection.

Marcia   We don't do that either.

Jermaine   But your question is vague.

Marcia   I shall rephrase, what precisely were those instructions?

Jermaine   To be happy.

Marcia   Thank you, Mister Adams.

Jermaine   But not to have her stick her nose in.

Marcia   The witness is excused.

Jermaine   All of the time.

Dawn   I object.

Jermaine   Your objection is noted. Can I go now please?

Dawn   If you must.

Jermaine   Laters.

Dawn   Don't 'laters' me like I'm one of the brers, now come here and give me a kiss.

Jermaine *does as he is told. He kisses* **Dawn** *and is then about to leave through the door when . . .*

Marcia   Am I a mirage?

Jermaine *does as he is told again.*

Jermaine   Now I'm gone.

Jermaine *leaves.*

Dawn   Do you remember that it was only yesterday Marse, when he was that sweet little five-year-old who would never leave my side? Who would bawl himself silly if I left his sight for only a second? Look pon him now.

Marcia   Not him. Can't be.

Dawn   Do you think he could be lying?

Marcia   So he can see *her?*

Dawn   I didn't say *her*. Did I say *her?*

Marcia   I can hear you thinking from here.

Dawn *then moves towards where* **Jermaine** *was sitting before he left and surveys.*

Marcia   What is this girl doing now?

Dawn   This is how Mum always knew when we were lying. She could always figure it out.

Marcia   Oh, behave yourself.

Dawn   Do you remember when you came home late one time?

Marcia   You will have to be a little more specific, Dawn.

Dawn   We were living on the estate then. You were going out with that *dregga dregga* white boy who lived below us.

Marcia   Jason Billing.

Dawn   He took you out for a *Wimpy* on the high road. You stayed out till gone six, on a school night. When you came home, you lied your arse off to Mum big time about being in detention and missing your bus.

Marcia   I did miss my bus.

Dawn   When she wanted to know the name of the teacher who was detaining you, you said Mister Clark. Ten seconds later, Mum sees Dad's shoes lying on the floor, and they were in your direct line of sight when you said the name *Clark*. What make of shoes were Dad's?

Marcia   *Clarks*, you little smart arse.

Dawn   There you go. What was it we used to call her?

Marcia   *Sherlock Mum.*

Dawn   We couldn't get anything past her.

Marcia   However, there is a little flaw in your summation there, Dawn. There actually was a teacher at school called *Mister Clark*.

Dawn   So what, you still chat lie.

Marcia   Dad's shoe made me think of him.

Dawn   I knew you remembered.

Marcia   Of course I remembered, Mum picked up that same shoe and beat me with it.

Dawn   Right, so where did this boy find the name *Lume* from?

Marcia   Did it occur he may be telling the truth?

Dawn   This is his line of sight.

Marcia   Dawn, hello?

Dawn   The coffee table.

Marcia   Why don't you let this go?

Dawn   You know something, don't you?

Marcia   Did I say?

Dawn   You are protecting him.

Marcia   No I'm not.

Dawn   Give it up girl, you know I won't stop with this. I have military grade intuition.

Marcia (*sighs*)   Mugs.

Dawn   Say?

Marcia   The coffee mugs. On the table.

Dawn *checks the underside of one of the mugs.*

Dawn (*reads*)   Lume!

Marcia   I got you those mugs when you bought the house.

Dawn   That lying crafty little wretch.

Marcia   Now, will you let this go?

Dawn   Big sister of mine, I aint even started.

Marcia   So he lied, only to get you off his back, he might not even want to see *her* again.

Dawn   So I just shut my mouth and stop being such a control freak.

Marcia   I didn't say that. Did I say that?

Dawn   I can hear you thinking from here.

Marcia *flashes her bra.* **Dawn** *roars with laughter.*

Tony *comes in, his hands are dripping wet.*

Dawn   You fix it?

Tony   There is something blocked down there. If you are planning on eating later, don't ask me what.

Dawn   Tony, don't come in here with your hands all wet, man. Dry them.

Tony   Yeah, the thought had occurred me to me, Dawn.

Tony *reaches for a kitchen towel. He tears off a piece to dry his hands.*

Tony   The game is still playing you nuh. You will have to call someone in to fix it.

Dawn   I do have someone on to fix it, his name is *Tony*.

Tony   Tell her to use the downstairs toilet from now on.

Dawn   I told you, she can't go downstairs no more.

Tony   What do you want me to do, Dawn? Pay to have a new toilet built upstairs right now for her?

Dawn   I want you to pay attention.

Tony   We're playing *Man U.*

Dawn   Selfish bastard.

Marcia   Have they scored yet?

Tony   *Ramsey* run for twenty yards, like his arse was on fire. He gave *Lacazette* him a quality cross, a sitter, how could he miss, how? Tired of this shit.

Tony *goes back inside.*

Marcia   So?

Dawn   I don't want to hear any of your *so's*, Marcia.

Marcia   How long is he here for this time?

Dawn   Mi say don't.

Marcia   Alright.

Dawn   And you can talk.

Marcia*'s phone rings.*

Marcia   Hi darling. Yes, you too, but I'm confused, well where are you? Oh God, no please. I told you, with Dawn. Yes I did, I did tell you *Giles*, look, just stay there, don't drive for God's sake. I'm coming, stay right there. I mean it, Giles, stay there. I'm coming, just hang on. (*Hangs up.*) Don't look at me, don't look at me like that.

Dawn   What is it now?

Marcia   He's been drinking, again. I have to go.

Dawn   So, go.

Marcia   I'm so sorry.

Dawn   It's alright.

Marcia   No it's not.

Dawn   So, why are you going if it's not?

Marcia   Dawn?

Dawn   Go on, out with you.

Marcia   You could have least made it hard for me.

Dawn   How am I supposed to do that?

Marcia   Call me a selfish cow. Say *that is so typical of you, Marse. You my sister or not?*

Dawn   Yer a selfish cow, that is so typical, Marse. You my sister or not?

Marcia   I'm serious.

Dawn   Well what do you want then? If you have to go, go.

Marcia   I'm worried about you.

Dawn   Backatcha.

Marcia   That is entirely different.

Dawn   I'm alright, honestly.

Marcia   I know you moving Mum in here with you was a big deal and I know I promised you things would be different from my end.

Dawn   Yeah, you did.

Marcia   And they will be. I'll make time for Mum, I'll make time for you, I'll do my share, I promise, but I must go now. Giles is waiting for me.

Dawn (*teasing*)   When the white man calls.

Marcia   Don't be like that.

Dawn   Oh just go.

Marcia   Love you.

Dawn   Yeah, yeah.

Tony *meets* **Marcia** *on the way out.*

Tony   Going already?

Marcia   I have to.

Tony   Just got here, man.

Marcia   And now I am going.

Tony   You know what we're going through.

Marcia   I believe so.

Tony   She's your mother as well.

Marcia   Thank you for pointing that out. I'm so glad you are here to tell me these things.

Dawn   Enough. Let her bounce, Tony.

Marcia   I'll call.

Dawn   You better.

Marcia   We'll do this again.

Dawn   I know, so go.

Marcia   I promise.

Dawn   Marse, don't make me slap you with my tits. Go if you're going.

Marcia   Love you.

Marcia *leaves.*

Dawn   Did they win?

Tony   Do dogs speak? Can't play the game, can't win shit. Fuck em!

Dawn   Tony!

Tony   There you go, you see, this always happens, every time she comes. Her and her fancy talk, and big ideas.

Dawn   You have a problem with the way I speak?

Tony   Just keeping you real, girl. Keeping you *street*.

Dawn   The shirt's looking a little tight.

Tony   Tight? Step off!

Dawn   You always put on some timber when you come back from tour.

Tony   A couple of pounds aint what I call timber. I aint like none of them brers you see now, you know back in the day, when they had summin going on for themselves. Nothing but slobs now.

Dawn   You dat.

Tony   With their bellies out to here, coming in and out of those nasty chicken shops, nah man!

Dawn   You dat!

Tony   Mi nuh dat, not now, not ever. Now bring yerself. Come here.

Dawn   Why would I want to do that?

Tony   Ca you are my puppy, that's why. You're still my puppy aren't you?

Dawn   Your what?

Tony   I just want to give you what all puppies want, you see.

Dawn   And what is that?

Tony   A bone.

Dawn (*laughs*)   No, you really did not say that.

Tony   I think I did. Come here, man.

Dawn   Why don't you just call the plumber yourself?

Tony   Say?

Dawn   Instead of always leaving everything for me to do?

Tony   Yes Dawn, kill the moment, why don't you?

Dawn   This is your as house as well.

Tony   Yet you decide all my yourself, to move your mother in here.

Dawn   Do you want her out?

Tony   Yes, Dawn, I want her out, fling her no good can't keep her shit in arse, out onto the street.

Dawn   Keep your voice down.

Tony   She can't do nuttin.

Dawn   You were God knows where.

Tony   Alright.

Dawn   Doing god knows to whom.

Tony   Enough, girl.

Dawn   She cannot take care of herself.

Tony   It was a surprise coming back, seeing her here. That is all.

Dawn   It wouldn't have been a surprise if you kept your phone on.

Tony   Can we stop now please, please. Look. My bone, that is.

Dawn   You call that a bone?

Dawn *grabs his crotch.*

Tony   Easy girl, watch the nails.

Dawn   *What all puppies want?*

Tony   You like it?

Dawn   Where you hear that?

Tony   I dunno, around.

Dawn   You said *puppies,* plural, not *puppy.*

Tony   Yeah, and so?

Dawn   Who are you on with it now?

Tony   No one girl, just you.

Dawn   Better be.

Tony   Believe.

Dawn   I am not joking this time.

Tony   Without a shadow.

Dawn   I aint putting up with any of that anymore.

Tony   See it deh! Yes, that's the Dawn I know.

Dawn   Believe dat.

Scene Two

Later that day, a park.

Jermaine   So, we meet again.

Simone   Yeah.

Jermaine   Two times in one week.

Simone   Unreal.

Jermaine   People will talk.

Simone   Although I should say the first time wasn't exactly a meet. More of a mutual glance.

Jermaine   I didn't mean to scare you.

Simone   Of all of the colleges that you had to pick, Jermaine.

Simone   Are you stalking me?

Jermaine   I'd thought you'd be glad to see me.

Simone   Answer my question.

Jermaine   What do you take me for? No, I am not stalking you. Two years it's been.

Simone   And yet here you are.

Jermaine   I am entitled to an education as well.

Simone   Don't let me stop you.

Jermaine   You look good.

Simone   Then I must be.

Jermaine   I missed you. (*Waits.*) Well?

Simone   What?

Jermaine   You're supposed to say you miss me.

Simone   Yes?

Jermaine   Well, do you?

Simone   Are you stupid, are you taking the piss here?

Jermaine   Alright.

Simone   I am trying to change my life here, I'm trying to get on.

Jermaine   Alright.

Simone   I never stopped thinking about you, happy?

Jermaine   Good. But I just had to tell my mum I was seeing someone else to keep her off the scent. I didn't want her to know I was meeting you.

Simone   She still blames me then? Don't answer. I don't know why I asked. I don't even care.

Jermaine   You don't?

Simone   Because you never told her the truth. Not one thing about her perfect golden boys. There it is, I saw it.

Jermaine   Saw what?

Simone   That look.

Jermaine   What look?

Simone   That disapproving look, that nose so far up yer own arse look. That *don't say that about my mum, you got no idea how it was her,* look.

Jermaine   Power down girl. I weren't.

Simone   You lie bad.

Jermaine   And you're getting all street again.

Simone   Cos of you. I hate you. I bloody hate you.

Jermaine   No you don't.

Simone   I bloody, bloody hate you.

Jermaine   I'll jog on then.

Simone   If you didn't want me here, you shouldn't have texted me.

Jermaine   You shouldn't have shown up like that, in the canteen.

Simone   Where else am I supposed to eat my lunch, Jermaine? All this time, every day, for two years, were you too afraid to call, hear my voice?

Jermaine   Something like that.

Simone   So what now then? I'm here, Jermaine, what now?

Jermaine   I should go.

Simone   Yes, one flash of the old Simone and you run.

Jermaine   I thought I was ready.

Simone   Now you're dashing me, again.

Jermaine   I thought I was ready for this, to see you.

Simone   You're seeing me now. Bastard man.

Jermaine   You can cuss me all you like.

Simone   Cuss you? You think I'm cussing you? Bwoi, you'll know when I'm cussing you.

Jermaine   Believe. (*Laughs.*)

Simone   What? What are you laughing at?

Jermaine   You. No matter what, you make me smile. I don't know how you do it

Simone   What are we doing?

Jermaine *takes her in his arms to console her.*

They kiss passionately but lovingly.

Simone   I wish I could forget all about you, I wish I could stop thinking about you.

Jermaine   Who do you think you are talking to?

Scene Three

Two weeks later.

The living room.

Tony   And that's it?

Dawn   Yes Tony, that is it.

Tony   She had a row with her man, and now she wants to come crying to you?

Dawn   Maybe he was knocking her about, I don't know.

Tony   She best the tell the police then, throw his arse out.

Dawn   It's his flat, Tony.

Tony   Of course it is.

Dawn   Shut up, man.

Tony   Tenner says his wife rocked up. She caught them at it, I bet you.

Dawn   My sister you mind?

Tony   It'll take him no time at all to go crawling back to wifey.

Dawn   She loves him.

Tony   Him love her?

Dawn   Well yeah.

Tony   He's going to look out for himself the same as any white man.

Dawn   As opposed to any man?

Tony   Hands and knees . . .

Dawn   You can stop now.

Tony   Begging for forgiveness mi tell you.

Dawn   You come like you are looking forward to it.

Tony   You are mad up in the head if you think that.

Dawn   It would be good for you.

Tony   How so?

Dawn   Another one of your *us versus them* tirades.

Tony   Are you saying you don't believe in any of that anymore?

Dawn   I'm not saying that.

Tony   So, what are you saying, Dawn? The white man is no longer the enemy, everything is sweet now, they love us, we love them, pull up a chair, why don't you?

Dawn   Alright, man.

Tony   Look at what they have been going on with, last couple of years.

Dawn   Oh hush.

Tony   Girl, they wouldn't blink twice about deporting yer mudda if you hadn't found her paperwork.

Dawn   Tony!

Tony   But to them, seventy years of hard graft in this country don't mean shit.

Dawn   Tony!

Tony   OK. Mouth shut.

Dawn   It's not even about that.

Tony   Marcia can tek care of Marcia, trust. Where was she, for Daryl?

Dawn   Where were you?

Tony   Right by your side, yu nuh see me? I weren't even that boy's dad.

Dawn   Oh for Christ . . .

Tony   You one tell me that every time his name comes up. At least I was there for the funeral, What about his own papa? Did his black arse rock up? I nuh see it.

Dawn   Yes that just evens this out for you, innit?

Tony   What you want then?

Dawn   Nothing. I do not want anything. Let's not do this, yeah. She's coming over, she's staying with us, that's it. Now I want to talk about Jermaine. The one who *is* your son, by the way.

Tony   What him do now?

Dawn   He's seeing her again. That what him do.

Tony   No chance.

Dawn   Maureen from across the road saw him in the park with some girl who, from the way she described, looks an awful lot like her.

Tony   OK then.

Dawn   OK? She a white gal, Tony. That alone should be more enough for you to mek noise. Me and him are having words when he comes in.

Tony   I have told him nuff times about how those kinds of white girls stay.

Dawn   You know that from experience do you?

Tony   Funny.

Dawn   Where are you going?

Tony   I got a rehearsal gig.

Dawn   But you said . . .

Tony   I know what I said. But Sammy needs a sax player ASAP, I did tell you this.

Marcia *enters.*

Dawn   So, you're leaving me again with all this?

Tony   I aint leaving you with anything, It's Jermaine's life, let him deal.

Marcia   Sorry.

Tony   For what?

Marcia   It was Jermaine who let me in.

Dawn   Jermaine, (*Shouts.*) Jermaine?

Marcia   I think he was going back out again.

Door slams.

Dawn (*calls*)   Yes ignore me, that go work. You and me boy go reach; I promise you that.

Marcia   Alright, what has he done?

Dawn (*to* **Tony**)   When are you back?

Tony   Late.

Tony *goes.*

Marcia   So what was that?

Dawn   Add it to the list.

Marcia   I appreciate this. I would have gone back to my flat, but I still have tenants there. They are moving out but not soon enough. I didn't know what else to do

Dawn   He's not flinging himself at you, is he?

Marcia   No, nothing like that.

Dawn   Him wife find out?

Marcia   No, Dawn.

Dawn   So what gives?

Marcia *removes her coat.* **Dawn** *hangs it up.*

Marcia   Dawn please, this is a real stressful time for me.

Dawn   Well begging yer pardon, *Massa!*

Marcia   This is serious.

Dawn   And as usual, I don't matter, yeah?

Marcia   Oh, come on!

Dawn   It's your drama that the world has to stop for.

Marcia   Dawn, I love him. I'm sorry he's not dark enough for you, but there you go.

Dawn   Him love you?

Marcia   What kind of a question is that? Of course he does.

Dawn   So, why are you here?

Marcia   Give me a minute, please?

Dawn *gestures* **Marcia** *to sit down.*

Marcia   So, what's happening with you?

Dawn   Are you seriously trying to change the subject?

Marcia   Tell me about your drama.

Dawn   I'm worried about Jermaine.

Marcia   You are always worried about Jermaine, he's fine.

Dawn   He's is not fine. He is with *her* again.

Marcia   After all of this time?

Dawn   A neighbour saw with him with her.

Marcia   You're not going to turn into a pillar of salt if you say her name you know, Dawn.

Dawn   She saw him, Marse. Only an hour after he stood here in this room, lying his arse off to me. To us! What the hell is he trying to do to me? Tony is back on the road in a couple of weeks, Mum won't eat what I give her.

Marcia   I'll go up.

Dawn   It's always me dealing with things.

Marcia   Did you not hear me? I said I will go up and see to her.

Dawn   You only just got here, rest up for a minute, what's up with you?

Marcia   Dawn?

Dawn   Dawn, what?

Marcia   We'll work it out.

Dawn   You can't work it out, you've got your own troubles, whatever they are.

Marcia   Do you want to die? I will leave you right here so, on this floor, bleeding. We will work it out girl, you and me. Now, if you don't mind *barkeep*, I would like the largest glass of red wine that you have available. I want it here, and I want it now. And seeing as no one else is around, what say you and I, do our *thing*?

Dawn   You mean spliff?

Marcia   Seriously, Dawn?

Dawn   Oh you mean the other *thing?*

Marcia   Yes, the other *thing.*

Dawn   Alright, no need to have a stroke. Your wish.

Marcia   Well, call it nuh!

Dawn   OK. *Alexa*, play kitchen playlist.

Dawn *goes inside the kitchen. Music plays.*

Marcia   Oh yes, thank the lawd.

Dawn *returns with a bottle of red and two glasses.*

Dawn   So, your drama, true talk now?

Marcia   He asked me to do something.

Dawn   Go on.

Marcia   The night I was last here, when he called me, when he was drunk.

Dawn   Continue.

Marcia   He had an accident in his car.

Dawn   *Alexa*, stop. Please don't tell me.

Marcia   No man. It was one of those pedestrian barriers on the road that he hit.

Dawn   Are you sure about that?

Marcia   Of course I'm bloody sure.

Dawn   How so? Were you in the car with him?

Marcia   Dawn, it was a pedestrian barrier, don't mek me repeat.

Dawn   Girl, you could have been hurt.

Marcia   Well I'm not, see me, standing here talking to you?

Dawn   Letting him drive though!

Marcia   Alright, but it's over, no harm done.

Dawn   Two weeks ago you say?

Marcia   It's over.

Dawn   So why are you here? Has something gone down? Come on, girl.

Marcia   He's a bloody MP, Dawn. He is one reshuffle away from being a cabinet minister.

Dawn   Finish up.

Marcia   Extra penalty points on his driving licence whilst driving under the influence is not a wise move for him do you not think?

Dawn (*realises*)   Have you gone *foo-fool* or something?

Marcia   I didn't think it could come to this.

Dawn   Come to what, Marse? Has it gotten out already?

Marcia   I don't know what you mean, sis, *I* was the one who was driving that night!

Dawn   If they can prove otherwise.

Marcia   They will not.

Dawn   That's your arse girl. Yer done.

Marcia   Thank you for pointing that out to me. *Alexa,* resume.

Dawn   *Alexa,* pause. He'll be alright, you won't.

Marcia   Please, Dawn.

Dawn   That is what I keep saying.

Marcia   Not again. *Alexa,* resume.

Dawn   *Alexa*, stop, That is the way them stay, those pale skins.

Marcia   And that is Tony talking. *Alexa*, resume.

Dawn   You see Tony here?

Marcia   With this on? Yer mad. I take he does not how intimate you were with *John Travolta* once?

Dawn   Oh, so you want to go there?

Marcia   Giles is still a good man, sis. He could do a lot of good for us.

Dawn   Pull my finger.

Marcia   As vivid as ever.

Dawn   Who else knows?

Marcia   I'm not sure.

Dawn   Who?

Marcia   A clerk from my chambers. She walked in on me speaking to Giles on the phone.

Dawn   Clerk's name?

Marcia   Jessica, Jaqueline, Janet! They all look the same with their *legally blonde* hair.

Dawn   Are you telling she's a '*Karen*'? How many times have I told you to watch out for them lot?

Marcia   If I have to hear Tony's *all white people are racist* chat again . . .

Dawn   This aint Tony, this is me . . .

Marcia   . . . I will hold you down, put a cushion over your face and *fart* on it. Mi nuh joke.

Dawn   They are not our friends, girl.

Marcia   You see this cushion in my hand Dawn?

Dawn   She's a bitch.

Marcia   She's had it in for me, ever since I wouldn't give her a reference.

Dawn   Double bitch.

Marcia   Her problem, not mine.

Dawn   A double lowdown privileged white *'Karen'* bitch.

Marcia   Sis!

Dawn   She wants putting out.

Marcia (*mimics*)   *She wants putting out!*

Dawn   Here it come.

Marcia   *Think yer a bit lemon now, do yer? Shall I turn on the custard? Do the Lambeth Walk? Lend us a pony!*

Dawn   Fine forget it, yer soff.

Marcia (*teases*)   And you're on the quiet. You have been watching those football hooligan films again, haven't you? You need to cut down, girl.

Dawn   I am only making a point.

Marcia   Your point is made.

Dawn   That it, that's all you have to say? *The point is made?*

Marcia   I'm not happy about this, if that what you *tink*.

Dawn   She is messing with your life.

Marcia   I don't know what's she's doing.

Dawn   *Work twice as hard to be as good, child!*

Marcia (*sighs*)   Oh without a doubt, the worst thing that generation had to tell us, the worst thing.

Dawn   You can't find room at all to cuss her?

Marcia   What difference would it make?

Dawn   Not a thing.

Marcia   Thank you.

Dawn   But do it anyway.

Marcia   Giles says I shouldn't worry

Dawn   But you are. He got you vex, innit? So, you rock up here. See, that is why I love you girl. Truly. Ca if that was me, I woulda caned that *Karen's claart* for even thinking about opening her mout.

Marcia   Listen to yourself, like you are back on the front line.

Dawn   Wa wrong wid dat?

Marcia   Nothing. For you, not a thing, just let me drink.

Dawn   You could at least tell me you are thinking about going downtown on her?

Marcia   What is this, Dawn, what is it really?

Dawn   Why do you think she's going to leak it? She's only saying what other people are going to be thinking. White people dem. *Who does she think she is, this uppity nig . . .?*

Marcia   No. Don't. Do not.

Dawn   You know they want to say it, girl. Every white person I know wants to say it. It must be making their piss boil that they can't say it, ca they want to say it.

Marcia   They don't all want to say it, Dawn.

Dawn   Deep down.

Marcia   . . . shut the fuc . . .

Dawn   Do you want me to fight her for you, Marse?

Marcia   What?

Dawn   Yes or no?

Marcia   You are being ridiculous.

Dawn   Lie bad. Marcia? Of course you do.

Marcia   I do not.

Dawn   Because you can't, because you're Miss Respectable now. Because you're a . . .

Marcia   *Sell-out?* Some horny married pale skin who aint getting it at home has now got himself the thirst for some *jungle fever* and I am happy to oblige?

Dawn   I didn't say that.

Marcia   But you want to say it. You know you want to say it, girl. Every black person I know wants to say it. It must be making their piss boil that they can't say it, ca they want to say it. Deep down/

Dawn   Alright, alright.

Marcia   You and Tony with your *I hate the white man for everything* bollocks! What do you think *John Travolta* would say if they heard you say that?

Dawn   Hey, first off, You leave *John* out of this. Second, if the white man had anything to with it, Mum's arse would be on a plane back to Jamaica.

Marcia   Will you get off that? Mum's papers checked out. She has indefinite leave to remain.

Dawn   But what if we couldn't have found them papers . . .?

Marcia   But you did. Mum kept her paperwork in order. She wasn't going anywhere, you know that, so please.

Dawn (*gives her the finger*)   Please this!

Marcia   *Alexa stop.* (*Music stops.*) OK, you want to do this, let's do this, get it out of your system?

Dawn   Pick a war, Marse . . .

Marcia   Boring!

Dawn   Pick any war, and any strife you care to mention, and you will find a white man . . .

Marcia   Boring!

Dawn   . . . at the heart if it, with the biggest spoon there is, stirring all kinds of shit.

Marcia   Oh Dawn, my love, I know enough about our *Karen*, if she ever did give me any more trouble.

Dawn   You are in trouble.

Marcia   All I have to do is text her civil servant fiancé, tell him all about a certain Christmas party, where a certain dutty twenty-eight-year-old was snorting the white as well as getting her tush well and truly pushed by a certain sixteen-year-old on work experience in the men's room. Now, you don't get that kind of power by mekin' a whole heap of noise on a demo through the streets of Hackney. Come back to me when you want to join the real world. It's her word against ours. *Alexa*, resume. (*Music returns.*)

Dawn   What if he had killed somebody?

Marcia   He didn't.

Dawn   Who is this Giles anyhow? Is he a dead spit for *Daniel Craig* or something? He had better have summin.

Marcia   He's five foot eight, wears glasses and supports *Kilmarnock*, wherever that is.

Dawn   And so? What him do for you?

Marcia   He noticed me.

Dawn   True say he did.

Marcia   He helped me. Do you think I would have made silk if it wasn't for his advice over the years, Dawn? You think Tony and his black power chat could sway that for me?

Dawn   Maybe if he had the same opportunities.

Marcia   Opportunities, mi backfoot!

Dawn   Hey, you felt the same as we once.

Marcia   I grew up. Not everything is about blasted race, Dawn.

Dawn   Most of the shit in this world is.

Marcia   Still boring!

Dawn   Just come out and say it, man.

Marcia   Say what?

Dawn   You prefer the white. The brothers don't do it for you.

Marcia   The ones I've dated, you're damn right. They all chat no end of rubbish like your man deh.

He told me that I was beautiful.

Dawn   You are beautiful. You don't need him to say that.

Marcia   Don't I?

Dawn   Nah man.

Marcia   Black women don't hear that enough you know, Dawn. Let alone most women.

Dawn   You chat shit.

Marcia   Name me the last time Tony said you were buff? (*Waits.*) See it deh. Like I've ever had time for a man, anyhow.

Dawn   You don't have time, mek time.

Marcia   Yes, *Mummy.* And I do make time. I make time for Giles.

Dawn (*teases*)   How many times a night?

Marcia   None of your damn business. Mind yourself.

Dawn   Pretty or not, I bet he'd run if he knew all about you.

Marcia   Let me guess, Craven Green?

Dawn   Does he know?

Marcia   I only told him what needs to know.

Dawn   Which means *fuck all* on your planet.

Marcia   As you wish.

Dawn   I still remember when we were kids; you and your scary ass temper, used to scare me something chronic. Out of control, don't even begin to describe it. One time, at school, whathername? Some little skinny white bitch.

Marcia   You and that word, man.

Dawn   Whathername, that bitch?

Marcia   Dial it down.

Dawn   . . . Too much to say for herself, right bully. The bitch Marse, whathername?

Marcia   Lawd Jesus . . .

Dawn   . . . Sarah . . . Sarah Curtis!

Marcia   Sarah Cooke.

Dawn   See it deh! I'd never seen so much blood. Never heard any one scream so loud.

Marcia   That is in the past, sis.

Dawn   Tell me to beat up on this *Karen's* arse and I will.

Marcia   Why are you doing this?

Dawn   I've always wanted to go one on with one of them, yu nuh? *A Karen.* Fling them down, clench my fist, tump the life.

Marcia   I'm here, aren't I?

Dawn   And don't even get me started on those *gammon* loving *Brexit* lot.

Marcia   Dawn?

Dawn   Come on, sis, let me bruc my foot off in her arse, just for you.

Marcia   I want to do my bit for Mum now.

Dawn   The Adams sisters, back on the front line.

Marcia   There is no front line!

Dawn   Love to kick arse.

Marcia   That time has gone, girl.

Dawn   Aint afraid to go all black on any one.

Marcia   It's over.

Dawn   Not for me.

Marcia   Stop it.

Dawn   No, you stop it. Stop it and hear me. *Alexa*, pause.

Music stops.

Dawn   Don't wave me off like one of your liberal ass white saviour mates chanting *Black Lives Matter* without the slightest idea why! You didn't just walk off the street; you had every right to be where you are, I've never known anyone, black or white, to hit them law books as hard as you did. You made silk all by yourself. Don't tell me this Giles fool is going to give up everything because of you. Don't tell me you don't want to bust that blonde Karen's wurtless claart right now. Because you not telling me, is you not trusting me, and that is insulting, girl. I don't deserve that.

Marcia   Do you still blame me for not being here for Daryl?

Dawn   You were never there.

Marcia   And where was Dad?

Dawn   Oh my word, the next person I love that does a deflection on me, I swear before God, I'm going to start a war.

Marcia   Dawn?

Dawn   You should have been here, Marse.

Marcia   You know I was away. I couldn't change my flight in time . . .

Dawn   You should have been here.

Marcia   I'm sorry, for the hundredth millionth rhatid blood claart time.

Dawn   Mum is dying.

Marcia   I know.

Dawn   It's happening, Marse. Soon. And I am the one that is going to find her. I'll go upstairs with her tea and cream crackers, and her pills, and I will be the one that finds her. Then I will do my round of phone calls starting with you. She may even be dead, right now.

Marcia   OK! Is it time for her pills? Let me.

Dawn   Don't worry yourself.

Marcia   She's my mother too.

Dawn   Are you going to tell her what's going on with you?

Marcia   That her eldest child could go to prison for lying her arse off? Yeah, why not, let's finish her off for good. Let's do it now. Want to watch?

Dawn *flashes her bra.* **Marcia** *does the same. They both laugh.*

Marcia *goes.*

Scene Four

Later that day.

The living room. **Dawn** *is showing* **Simone** *in.*

Dawn   You look nervous.

Simone   I'm fine.

Dawn   Good.

Simone   I've started college. Same as Jermaine. I didn't know. I swear.

Dawn   Well done.

Simone (*surprised*)   Are you praising me?

Dawn   Why don't you sit down.

Simone   Media Studies.

Dawn   Is that right?

Simone   I like it. Jermaine told me once, about me having a brain, and it's time I used it.

Dawn   You should be going because it is what you want.

Simone   It is what I want.

Dawn   Good.

Simone   Maybe I can be like your sister, politics and that.

Dawn   She's a barrister. You will need a law degree, you said Media Studies.

Simone   I know I meant, actually . . . I mean I didn't mean.

Dawn   What?

Simone   I don't know. I don't know what to say. I don't know what I mean.

Dawn   Clearly.

Simone   What do you want me to say?

Dawn   What do you think I want you to say?

Simone   That I'm sorry?

Dawn   Are you sorry?

Simone   Is that why you called me?

Dawn   Not exactly.

Simone   Because I am. I am so bloody sorry.

Dawn (*cuts in*)   I called you because I want you to stop seeing him.

Simone   Well, that was quick.

Dawn   Why waste time?

Simone   The thing is, I don't think I can do that.

Dawn   What?

Simone   I know I can't. I've tried.

Dawn   What the hell do you think this is?

Simone   I love him. That's what it is.

Dawn   Don't you dare.

Simone   Why are you asking me this?

Dawn   Because it will be the same as it was before.

Simone   It does not have to be.

Dawn   You cannot stand the sight of me. You never have.

Simone   I liked you when I first met you.

Dawn   I cannot say I have ever liked you much.

Simone   Even when we first met?

Dawn   Especially when we first met.

Simone   I wonder why that is.

Dawn   You can think what you like.

Simone   Why are you doing this to me, why can't you give me a chance?

Dawn   Are you going to stop seeing him or not?

Simone   I'm trying to be nice; that is possible, you know? Nice! Thought you and me could be tight.

Dawn   Tight? Like when you were with those boys that beat my son to death?

Simone   Oh come on.

Dawn   That kind of tight?

Simone   Please?

Dawn   Please, what?

Simone   I can't go through all of that again with you.

Dawn   You can't?

Simone   I really can't.

Dawn   Like you are the only one who is hurting here.

Simone   I know I am not.

Dawn   This gal!

Simone   You are not listening to me.

Dawn   What do you have that is worth listening to?

Simone   I didn't know they were going to do that.

Dawn   Of course you didn't

Simone (*snaps*)   You wanna know who you really should chat to, Dawn? (*Almost says* **Jermaine**'s *name but changes her mind.*) Never mind. Nothing but a waste of time here, I should give you what you want, innit?

Dawn   Do as you like.

Simone   *Yeah, nasty dirty white trash, Simone, what she do, go corrupt those two sweet looking black boys?*

Dawn   Why Daryl? Why Jermaine?

Simone   It was always Jermaine.

Dawn   So Daryl was what? Someone you just used to pass the time?

Simone   It weren't like that. How many more times?

Dawn   You've done enough damage to my family. Go find someone else to lay down with. Deh must be plenty.

Simone   Some one white?

Dawn   Do you want money?

Simone   Shame.

Dawn   How much? I'm serious. How much will it take.

Simone   Yer sick, well and truly. Should be put to sleep for even thinking it. You wonder why Daryl hated you.

Dawn   Lies.

Simone   He couldn't stand you, man.

Dawn   Nothing but lies.

Simone   When we were lying in bed, naked, arms all over each other . . .

Dawn   Nasty little . . .

Simone   He would tell me, he would cuss you night and day about how much he loathed you . . .

Dawn *lunges at* **Simone**, *grabbing her by the throat.*

Dawn   You think you know? What is it, what is it that you think you know? Cos you went to the same school as my boys, cos you can chat like us, you think that makes you black? Are you mad? Let me tell you this right now, what I am doing, this is been black, everything inside of me, and more, more than your dumb arse cheap white self couldn't even imagine.

Dawn *realises she has gone too far. She releases* **Simone**.

Dawn   Just stay away.

Simone *grabs her bag, dashes out.*

Scene Five

Later in the day.

The living room.

Dawn   Can you believe that girl, the brass neck!

Tony (*chuckles*)   Dawn going downtown and more.

Marcia   Yeah you go and laugh it up.

PC Spencer   She still maintains that you assaulted her. Did you?

Dawn (*mocks*)   Assault?

Marcia   Is that a yes?

Dawn   Look, PC?

PC Spencer   Spencer.

Dawn   *Spencer? Spencer? Spencer? Spencer?* Look at me.

PC Spencer   I beg your pardon?

Dawn   Look pon. *Spencer?* You're not from the same *Spencer's* who used to live on Mayford Road back in the day, are you? *Doreene Spencer?*

PC Spencer   My aunt. She still lives there.

Dawn   Move yerself! *Doreene Spencer* is your auntie!

PC Spencer   She is my second cousin actually, but we all grew up calling her *Auntie,* you know.

Dawn   Respect your elders, yeah we know. I knew it, I knew there was something the minute you breezed yourself in here. I could see it in yer face. You got her look. The *Spencer* look! How is Doreene? She good?

PC Spencer   She's very good. She's a grandmother now.

Dawn   Lord Jesus!

PC Spencer   Twice.

Dawn   She proud of you?

Marcia   Dawn, don't?

PC Spencer   Is there a problem?

Dawn   No problem with me, PC. The only thing is, I can still remember Doreene and myself, on the front line

Marcia   The girl does not need to hear this.

PC Spencer   I am not a girl. I am a police constable.

Marcia   OK.

Dawn   It was me, your aunt and her brothers, all on the frontline throwing brick, and lawd knows what else, at the beast, the Babylon. Brixton first, then *Broadwater*, a week later. What, you don't know about *Broadwater Farm?* Look it up, girl.

PC Spencer   Now look.

Dawn   That's your history.

PC Spencer   I know what it is.

Dawn   So, I ask again, is she proud of you?

PC Spencer   Doreene is my aunt, not my mother. But I would like to think that she is. And yes I know all about *Broadwater Farm.*

Dawn   Then you should know about those white colleagues of yours, one of whom was sitting where you are right now, telling me, to my face, *There is no evidence to suggest it was a racist attack.*

Marcia (*to* **Tony**)   Are you just going to stand there?

Tony   Let her speak.

Dawn   Eye witnesses heard those white boys calling my sons black this, black that from one end of the street to the next, no evidence?

PC Spencer   I am aware of the allegations made against that officer.

Dawn   Allegations? You know, you may look, but you don't come like a Spencer, if I may say.

PC Spencer   I also know that there are men in prison, serving a life sentence each for what they did to your son.

Dawn   Two men! The other one is strutting around somewhere, breathing free air as we chat.

PC Spencer   Perhaps we should return to the matter in hand?

Dawn   All I did was grab her.

PC Spencer (*writing notes*)   I see.

Dawn   Nuh, you don't *see*.

Marcia   Dawn, stop it ?

Dawn   Could you stop writing for a minute please, please stop writing and listen, can you do that? Erm . . .

PC Spencer (*stops writing*)   *Ayesha.*

Dawn   Thank you, *Ayesha*. We were just having an argument, things got a little heated, and that was all.

PC Spencer   Are you saying you were provoked *by* Miss Norris?

Dawn (*snaps*)   Gal get right into my face, what was I supposed to do . . .

Marcia   OK, we should stop, right now.

Dawn   I was provoked by her.

Tony   She provoked her! Write that down, *Ayesha*.

PC Spencer   Ms Adams, did Miss Norris strike you first? I should say, lying to me right now is not a good idea.

Tony   Yes cos she one has to be lying.

Marcia You are not helping, Tony.

Tony Look at what they've got you doing girl, to your own people.

PC Spencer (*ignoring him*) Ms Adams?

Dawn No. It was all me. She said something I didn't like, I lost it. I grabbed her, alright?

PC Spencer Right. I think that is all I need for now.

Tony So, what happens now, you go arrest her?

Marcia Yes, you would love that. Back on the streets. Placards and loudspeakers for you.

PC Spencer I should warn you, Ms Adams, a formal charge is entirely possible. But it's not my decision. Miss Norris was the one who issued the complaint. It is up to her if she decides to press charges. Why don't I leave it for the day, I shall give her a call tomorrow? In the meantime, Ms Adams, you might want to use this time to reflect? Sounds to me, all she is looking for is an apology. Do you understand what I mean? I best be going.

Marcia I'll walk you out.

PC Spencer (*curt*) No, I'm fine.

Marcia Is there a problem, Constable?

PC Spencer Not at all, but I know the way out.

Marcia Alright then.

Dawn Give your aunt my best. (*Clenches then raises her fist.*) Tell her to keep swinging. She'll know what I mean.

PC Spencer As do I. Good day, Ms Adams.

Spencer *exits*.

Dawn A Spencer! In police uniform. That is almost a contradiction in terms. Can you believe that?

Dawn *can feel* **Marcia**'s *glare from the other side of the room.*

Dawn   What?

Marcia   I can smell the spliff from over here, Dawn.

Tony   Just a little weed, to calm her nerves.

Marcia   And yours?

Dawn   It's no big deal, Marse. If it was, *Juliet Bravo* deh would have said summin.

Marcia   Or maybe she is more of a *Spencer* than you think. How many lives do you think you have, girl?

Marcia   You should apologise.

Dawn   To that skank? Ask me another.

Marcia   For God's sake!

Tony (*rolls a spliff*)   Is that your plan?

Marcia   What do you have then, big man?

Tony   No woman of mine . . .

Marcia   . . . woman of yours?

Tony   . . . is going running after some low class wigga, who as good as put our boy in the ground.

Marcia   Daryl was not your boy. Jermaine is, or have you spent so long out of their lives, you forgotten who is who?

Dawn   Hey, that is hitting way below the belt now, Marse.

Marcia   Wa wrong wid yu? You want to go to jail?

Dawn   Here she come, my Craven Green sis.

Marcia   How many more times do you want me to keep saying I'm sorry?

Dawn   Voice down, you'll wake Mum.

Marcia   Ten? Twenty? Five hundred? How many? Gimme a number.

Dawn   I need some air.

Marcia   Dawn!

Dawn   Leave me alone, man.

Marcia   Oh so now you are running. (*Calls.*) What are you going to do about this?

Dawn *leaves*.

Marcia (*to* **Tony**)   You know you could help, instead of always encouraging her.

Tony   She's entitled to her own mind.

Marcia   Her mind is in the past; it is of no use to her now.

Tony   So you say, so you feel.

Marcia   My God, you are lazy.

Tony   Cos I don't get as wound up as you?

Marcia   Gimme that.

Tony   Say that again?

Marcia   Just pass me it.

Tony *hands over the spliff.* **Marcia** *deliberately stubs it out.*

Tony   Backside!

Marcia   Was that you taking her back to *Broadwater*? Were you even there, Tony?

Tony   This look like a court room to you? You in my yard!

Marcia   That's funny, I could have sworn the mortgage was under my sister's name.

Tony   I remember plenty about Broadwater. The front line!

Marcia   And I remember the Spencers. Bad lot every one of them, most, if not all, did time, even Doreene.

Tony   Is there a point coming?

Marcia   And I remember your family, your dad. The great *Dennis Collins*.

Tony   What about him?

Marcia   *Black power! Haile Selassie! Blood ah go run, till justice come!*

Tony   What of it, Marcia?

Marcia   He helped set up that youth club for the black kids in the church hall.

Tony (*boasts*)   Yeah, yeah, he did.

Marcia   You played table tennis, I used to watch, you were good. You won medals, right?

Tony   And?

Marcia   There was a picture of you and him in the local paper. Your precious dad who would lie down in traffic for his black community.

Tony   Believe that.

Marcia   Thing is, I wonder what the impact would be if there was picture of me fighting him off nuff times, when he tried to put his hand up my skirt.

Tony   Hey!

Marcia   Not just me though, any girl that passed his way, ask Dawn if you don't believe, him and his black power brers. *Hey pretty gal, where yu go?*

Tony   You got jokes.

Marcia   *Yu want free it up?*

Tony   Mind what yer saying about my dad please?

Marcia It's alright, calm yourself.

Tony I am calm. Just show some respect.

Marcia Tony, I'm not about to shout out *Me Too* from the top of my voice just because some dutty old man tried it on. I could handle him. But spare me the good old days when the fight was on, *666, that's the sound of the police*, all a' that, alright? Spare my sister. Because she does not need that right now.

Tony Well, that is a lot of chat coming from a fully paid-up emergency black friend whose just had her arse thrown under a bus.

Marcia I haven't been thrown under anything.

Tony Give him time, girl. It's happening.

Marcia What is it, Tony, what is your problem with me?

Tony *Queen Charlotte*, that was your school?

Marcia Really?

Tony Every day, quarter to four, a whole of them, maybe even you, used get the same bus as us. All of you, with your *hoity toity my shit don't stink* vibe.

Marcia And you went to *Beckett Row* where every brer I know who went to that school no longer has a single tooth in their mouth that is their own. Every school in the whole of south was *hoity toity* compared to *Beckett*. And for your information, because I think I know where you are trying to go with this, I did not go to *Queen Charlotte*.

Tony *St Jude's* then.

Marcia *Craven Green for Girls*, do you ever listen to what your woman has to say?

Tony So, she my woman now?

Marcia Do you?

Tony   *Craven Green*. With the burgundy uniform?

Marcia   That was us.

Tony   Yeah, the bus driver would always go past your stop. You lot was rough man.

Marcia   The roughest. We'd piss on *Beckett Row*.

Tony   Oh, is this you showing off now?

Marcia   Would it surprise you if I said I was expelled?

Tony   You?

Marcia   Yes?

Tony   Explain.

Marcia   Never mind.

Tony   No, come on.

Marcia   Forget it, I shouldn't have brought it up, it's a long story.

Tony   I like long stories.

Marcia   Go and find Dawn.

Tony   In a minute. Let me hear this. What you afraid of?

Marcia   I hit a teacher.

Tony   That's it?

Marcia   Miss Grayling, she was a racist bitch, lecturing me on and on, about my short ass temper, I couldn't take it.

Tony   Gwan, Marcia!

Marcia   I crushed her nose like an egg. One punch. That was all it took. My last day at Craven Green for Girls. Shocked?

Tony   No.

Marcia   Why?

Tony   She had it coming. Tell me, true talk now, when you were pounding Miss Grayling's face, how did you feel?

Marcia   Ashamed of course.

Tony   You're lying. What are you scared of, Marcia?

Marcia   I am not scared.

Tony   Come on, tell me. Did it feel good?

Marcia   No. It didn't.

Tony   Come on, girl. True talk.

Marcia   It felt bloody good.

Tony   See it deh.

Marcia (*lets slip*)   Damn right. Ah, shit.

Tony   There it goes.

Marcia   What?

Tony   The wall you put between us.

Marcia   There is no wall.

Tony   Sorry, wrong end of the stick.

Marcia   Have you forgotten all about the mother of your child, my sister?

Tony   How about we change the subject?

Marcia   Please try.

Tony   She looks at me sometimes, like it's my fault, for Daryl.

Marcia   You weren't here.

Tony   I was here when it counted, when it mattered, so you can stop yer noise yeah, you weren't around either when the Babylon showed up to tell her first born was dead. She had to deal with that all on her own. It's like I have to use everything in me, not to get her in a headlock, say 'stop yer noise, gal'. (*Sees her face.*) I didn't say I would.

Marcia   Do you expect me to sympathise?

Tony   Absolutely not. Rt. Honourable Marcia Adams.

Marcia   I am not an MP in court, I am addressed as *Ms Adams*. My colleagues refer to me as *My Learned Friend*.

Tony   Wow! All that shit really means something to you doesn't it? I am sexually aroused, my *Learned Friend*.

Marcia   I am going to find my sister now.

Tony   Or you could stay, either way I don't mind, but do it because you want to, yeah.

Marcia   What have you got me down as, Tony? What do you see? What do you think?

Tony   It still matters to you, don't it? Still living your life according to their rules.

Marcia   At least I am in the room.

Tony   You are only in the room cos they are now giving you permission to be in the room, but they are still the same people who didn't want you in the room there in the first place. I think you're lost, girl, you and your kind. That is what I think.

Marcia   You don't know anything about me.

Tony   Who are you, Marcia, who are you really? To them? Tell me what you want?

Marcia *goes to leave.* **Tony** *grabs her arm.*

Tony   What do you both want?

Marcia   Do you mind?

Tony   I don't know what she wants from me.

Marcia   Yeah you do.

Tony *kisses her.*

Tony   Was I your first, Marcia? Back in the day?

Marcia   Before you chose my sister?

Tony   Black man, Marse? Was I your first, black man? (*Giggles.*) I bet there aint been one since.

Marcia   You are cheap, Tony. Everything about you is cheap. Back then, right now.

Tony   What do you think Dawn would . . .

Marcia   Dawn don't know about us. She will never know.

Tony   Are you so sure?

Marcia   Like you are man enough to tell her. Because you have got yourself a sweet thing going on here, you always have. Months on the road, a nice yard and a bed whenever you need it. A woman just eager to free it up, you probably only need to do her just the once for every visit, who else would wanna touch it?

Tony   Hey, I never thought of her like that.

Marcia   Yes you have, I know you have, don't lie to me.

Tony   Have you?

Marcia   She is worth twenty of me, and fifty of you.

Tony   Damn coconut.

Marcia   Is that all you have?

Tony   You think you know me?

Marcia   Your cute boyish good looks are starting to fade now, as well as your alluring six pack.

Tony   You noticed.

Marcia   You couldn't be anything like your *black power* dad.

Tony   I never wanted to be like him.

Marcia   I bet. Those expectations were way too high for you, innit?

Tony   Is that what *you* have? Some father son bullshit?

Marcia   You were nothing but a five-minute fumble, at a blues party, and that is it. But thanks for the chat, it was nice, now I am going to go and find my sister.

Tony   I was still here when she lost Daryl, Marcia. Where were you?

Marcia   I couldn't change my flight.

Tony (*does not believe a word of that*)   Couldn't yer?

Marcia *goes.*

Scene Six

Later that evening.

The living room.

Dawn *comes in with bags of shopping.*

Dawn (*calls*)   Mum, I'm back. I got your tea and crackers, I'll be up in a second, yeah. Jermaine? Tony?

Dawn *does a quick survey to check that the coast is clear.*

Survey complete. It is!

Dawn (*excited*)   Alexa, play *Take That.*

Music plays.

Dawn *starts putting away the groceries. She dances along as well as sings. She is well into it.*

There is a loud thud from upstairs.

Dawn   Mum?

Dawn *dashes upstairs.*

The music continues to play.

A short while later, **Dawn** *returns, in tears.*

She wanders aimlessly around the room, not having any idea what to do with herself.

She finally manages to compose herself and finds enough strength to find her phone.

Dawn   *Alexa*, off.

Music stops.

Dawn *finds a number. She waits for* **Marcia**.

Dawn   She's gone, Marse.

End of Act One.

Act Two

Scene One

Three weeks later. It is 2 am.

Marcia *sits alone as she speaks with* **Giles** *on the phone.*

Marcia Well, that's it then, isn't it? If they have proof, they have proof, yes that is it. Yes, I imagine you would be. I'm feeling a little sorry myself. Oh, and I am fine by the way. (*Full of sarcasm.*) (*Sighs.*) My mother, Giles. Tomorrow, or should I say, this morning. Yes, yes, you have. No, no. I'm not angry at all. It's getting late. I need to go soon and get some sleep, if that is at all possible, well . . . hang on, I didn't mean right . . . (**Giles** *hangs up.*) . . . now. *Yes, I love you as well, with all of my heart, Marcia.* Love me, mi backfoot!

Scene Two

Later that morning.

Jermaine *is with* **Simone** *on the park bench. He is opening a card.*

Jermaine There is a stamp on it.

Simone I was going to post it.

Jermaine Why didn't you?

Simone I didn't want your mum to see it.

Jermaine You think she would have opened it?

Simone Well, there's a chance.

Jermaine True that. (*Looks at the front of the card.*) I like it.

Simone It's a condolence card, Jermaine, you are not supposed to like it.

Jermaine Alright, I hate it then. It's the ugliest condolence card I've ever seen.

Simone I'm glad you called me. I didn't think you would after what your mum did, but I'm glad.

Jermaine Mum has a lot on. It's not your fault what happened.

Simone Not my fault?

Jermaine Her mum, my gran.

Simone Right.

Jermaine So, don't worry about Mum.

Simone I won't, as long as you say.

Jermaine *inspects the picture on the card again.*

Jermaine Why birds?

Simone Come again?

Jermaine Mum has been getting a lot of cards with birds on them. What do birds have to do with death?

Simone It looked nice to me; it was the best I could find.

Jermaine Not your fault, Simone.

Simone Why would it be my fault. Jermaine?

Jermaine It isn't. I just find interesting that the people who made this card, choose to signify birds with death, are the birds that are flying supposed to be taking souls to heaven or something?

Simone It could be.

Jermaine Mum got one just like this.

Simone I wish I could be with you, today.

Jermaine One sight of you and Mum will drop in the same grave as gran's.

Simone Just make sure you mind yourself. Drink water.

Jermaine Water?

Simone   I know, it sounds mad, but make sure you drink lots of water. I found that when my gran died, Dad was dehydrated. He was so busy taking care of things, he wasn't taking proper care of himself, so please do that, yeah? Please take care of yourself.

Jermaine   Don't worry yourself about me. I got Mum.

Simone   But I do worry myself about you, so tough, deal with it.

Jermaine   Simone, she was ninety-one! She had a good long life. Me and Mum have got this.

Simone   But she was still your gran.

Jermaine   But not my mum.

Simone   Alright, what is this?

Jermaine   Say?

Simone   What are you doing, Jermaine?

Jermaine   Excuse?

Simone   Cos if you mention your mum one more time in a sentence, I'm going to beat you around the head with summink.

Jermaine   What are you kicking off about, I don't understand?

Simone   You are doing it again

Jermaine   What?

Simone   Trying to be like your brother.

Jermaine   I'm not.

Simone   Playing me, going around and around, messing with my feelings.

Jermaine   Messing?

Simone   Until he finally gets what he wants. What do you want, Jermaine?

Jermaine   Simone?

Simone   What do you want? Tell me.

Jermaine (*comes clean*)   You can't press charges.

Simone   I knew it. I bloody knew.

Jermaine   Mum's been through enough, please Simone?

Simone   Have you seen this bruise on my neck?

Jermaine   I know.

Simone   Do you?

Jermaine   She's not as tough as she thinks she is.

Simone   Tough enough, I'd say.

Jermaine   Please Simone?

Simone   And if I don't. What?

Jermaine   What, nothing.

Simone   Are you telling me, are we done now? Again?

Jermaine   You are not listening, man.

Simone   I spoke to the feds already, Jermaine. You really thought I was going to press charges didn't you? You think I would do that to your mum? I just wanted to scare her, man. I don't business she's had it tough, that don't give her the right to treat me like trash it don't give anyone the right, not her, not Daryl, you get?

Jermaine   I get.

Simone   I wanted her to know.

Jermaine   That her own son hated her guts?

Simone   Jermaine, he did. He told me.

Jermaine   I know that.

Simone   So, why are you sweating me for, you got what you wanted, so go, jog on. It's what yer good at.

Jermaine   Hold up.

Simone   For what?

Jermaine   I don't think your trash. I love you.

Simone   Daryl said that, over and over to me.

Jermaine   He was lying to you.

Simone   I did come out of school with four A levels, you know Jermaine. I know he was lying. I was nothing but *a taste of the white*, yeah?

Jermaine   Simone?

Simone   Are you going to jog on now or shall I? You got what you wanted, man.

Jermaine   Have I? Is that a joke or summin?

Simone   Well that's on you, I can't help you with that.

Jermaine   I'll tell her.

Simone   Little Jermaine, Mum's golden boy.

Jermaine   Daryl said that.

Simone   I know he said that.

Jermaine   Well don't, please?

Simone   I'll be thinking of you today.

Jermaine   I'll tell her. I will tell Mum the truth.

Simone   No, you won't. Drink water.

Scene Three

The living room. Later that day.

Dawn, *dressed in black enters. She is in a foul mood. She pours herself a glass of rum.*

Dawn   Lying lowdown, dutty, skank . . .!

Without any instruction from **Dawn***, the Alexa turns itself on and plays Harry Belafonte's 'Jamaica Farewell.'*

Dawn   Say? *Alexa*, off. *Alexa*, off. *Alexa!*

Alexa continues to play.

Dawn   Listen yeah, I aint in the mood for your shit today, mi say off!

Alexa continues to play.

Dawn   Oh, you want play. Where's that chord?

Dawn *goes to pull the chord out when* **Sylvia** *comes from downstairs. She slowly walks around the room, singing along to Jamaica Farewell.* **Dawn** *is aghast to see her mother here.*

Sylvia *takes a seat.*

Sylvia   *Alexa, off.*

Alexa stops.

Sylvia *waits.*

Sylvia   Hey, child.

Dawn *quickly pours herself another glass of rum. She downs it in one then she stares at her mother.*

Sylvia   Are you just going to stand there? Say something, nuh?

Dawn   What the actual fuck?

Sylvia   You should not swear. It disempowers you. What else?

Dawn (*reciting to herself*)   Sylvia Rosemary Crosby Adams, was born in Jamaica in a village called Frankfield on the seventeenth of March, 1928.

Sylvia   St Patrick's Day. You forget to say that at the church.

Dawn   She had four older sisters, and three younger brothers, or was it three younger sisters, four older brothers?

Sylvia   You were right the first time.

Dawn   Her father was a tailor, he moved around a lot. All over the island. Her mother stayed at home, earning money on the side as a seamstress.

Sylvia   What are you doing, child?

Dawn   Reminding myself that you are dead. And you cannot be here. (*Recites.*) She spent much of her childhood in Kingston with her aunt *Miriam* with whom she went to live with her when she was three years old and went back to her live with her parents when her aunt died.

Sylvia   I was twelve.

Dawn   You were twelve.

Dawn *pours herself another glass of rum.*

Sylvia   Don't drink like it is water.

Dawn   Come on, Dawn, you are losing it girl. Hold it together.

Dawn *shuts her eyes. She waits a few seconds before opening them.* **Sylvia** *is still there.*

Dawn   Jesus Christ. You are not here. You are not really here.

Sylvia   Well of course I am not *really* here.

Dawn   It's the rum. I need to cut down.

Sylvia   Clearly.

Dawn   Good. Well, you can fuck off then.

Sylvia   Watch your mouth for me, please?

Dawn   Or what?

Sylvia   Don't talk to me so.

Dawn   What are you going to do, Mummy? Beat me with one of your slippers? Tell me to go stand in the corner?

Sylvia   You're the one who wants me.

Dawn   I remember this one time, I needed to pee, so bad, I was what, nine? You didn't believe me, you made me stay in the corner. I can't even remember what I did, but I know I was about nine. I had to cross my legs, real tight. You made me wet myself.

Sylvia   Dawn?

Dawn   I will always be thinking about you, I can't help that. Is that the way it's going to be from now on? Every time you pass my mind, you are just going to rock up like this?

Sylvia   The thought had occurred.

Dawn   Well, you know what you can do with that thought. Are you trying to drive me mad here?

Sylvia   Have you finished?

Dawn   It's been a long day, that's all, a very long day. You're not here.

Sylvia   So let me go.

Dawn   I need to tek my mind off. Boom! (*Calls.*) *Alexa*, play *ABBA*.

Alexa   *Am sorry, I didn't quite get that . . .*

Dawn   Oh, for Christ sake, Alexa, play some bloody *ABBA*, man, now!

Alexa   *Am sorry, I didn't quite get that . . .*

Dawn   Shut the fuck up, *Alexa!*

Sylvia   Language, please?

Dawn   You can shut up too.

Sylvia   Why are you so angry?

Dawn   Are you trying to be funny?

Sylvia   Stop it.

Dawn   You could have waited.

Sylvia   For what?

Dawn   To die of course. There was so much . . . that I needed . . . to say . . . you know what, just forget it.

Sylvia   Why do you have me looking like this?

Dawn   You showed me a photo of you once. It was my favourite picture of you. You were so full of life and thin! You really had it going on for yourself.

Sylvia   Thank you, Madame.

Dawn   Those hips! No wonder Dad made a beeline for you.

Sylvia   Well of course he did.

Dawn   I wasn't even a glint in your eye then was I?

Sylvia   Yer telling me. To this day, I still have no idea how you got here.

Dawn   Would like me to draw you a picture?

Sylvia   You always were such a nasty little girl.

Dawn   Is that why you used to beat us, Mum?

Sylvia   There is no need to go over that.

Dawn   Cos you never wanted us in the first place?

Sylvia   I beat you both because you were renk.

Dawn   There were times I think you enjoyed it.

Sylvia   Don't talk foolishness. Was I supposed to let the two a' yu grow up like a tree?

Dawn   You didn't deserve our love.

Sylvia Maybe not, but you and your sister have buried me, all the same.

Dawn Everyone is coming here soon.

Sylvia I know, so fix yourself, come on.

Dawn I don't know what to say to them.

Sylvia You said plenty at the church. What is it? Tell me what you need to know.

Dawn What you mean right here, right now?

Sylvia As good as time as any.

Dawn (*chuckles*) *As good as time as any?* Oh Mummy, you got jokes.

Sylvia Tell me what you want, child?

Dawn I honestly don't know how to do that.

Sylvia My fault?

Dawn Partly, yeah.

Sylvia Thank you for that.

Dawn You asked.

Sylvia Jermaine? Is he alright?

Dawn I don't know what to do about him.

Sylvia I can't help you with that.

Dawn Then why ask, and why not?

Sylvia Because it is not what you want.

Dawn Don't tell me what I want.

Sylvia You want somebody to blame, me. I know you better than you know yourself. Yer fudda and I are were only people, Dawn.

Dawn No you were not.

Sylvia   So what are we then?

Dawn   You were Mum and Dad.

Sylvia   So we were not allowed to mess up? Yer fart. I could have been a better person. I coulda have more.

Dawn (*correcting her*)   *Should* have been better, Mum! *Should* have done more! I don't even want to talk about that. We are not discussing you.

Sylvia   Alright then.

Dawn   You lot, you had your time.

Sylvia   Our time? Is that how you would describe our life here?

Dawn   See, alright I know you're getting angry.

Sylvia   You know nothing! Nothing! You hear me? I know it seem we nuh give yu much, Dawn.

Dawn   It don't seem, it is.

Sylvia   Well, it's just too bad.

Dawn   That's it? That's yer help?

Sylvia   Yer all that's left. Our history . . .

Dawn (*cringes*)   Oh man.

Sylvia   Listen to me, our history, future is in yer hands deh.

Dawn   Yeah, yeah, you see, I know wass coming awready. We have no idea how hard it was fer yu all. *No blacks, no Irish, no dogs*, in every winder, in all the streets, when are you lot gonna move away from dat, when are you gonna give us summin new, summin else?

Sylvia   Have you see any of *our lot*, lately, Dawn? Most, if not all of us, are dead already. Have you not noticed? Or do you not care? You are as bad as they.

Dawn   *They?*

Sylvia   White people, dem so! We are going, child, every single one of us that first come here. Why this country is in such a hurry now to send us all back home is a mystery to me. We go all die, no one blasted well cares about us anyhow, just sit down and wait nuh! Why the hell they feel they need to frighten us like this, I do not know.

Dawn   Whose getting renk now?

Sylvia   Stop using us as an excuse. You are afraid. You're scared to death and you know it. You're no better than me.

Dawn   I never told my boys that I wish I had aborted them. Those words have never left my lips.

Sylvia   Fair enough.

Dawn   *Fair enough* she says.

Sylvia   Look, I said what I said, but what do you really want from me?

Dawn   I never knew you. You never let me in.

Sylvia   You are looking in the wrong place, Dawn. It's down to yu pickne now, to tek what we got, for better or for worse, and build on it.

Dawn   Blah, blah, bloody blah.

Sylvia   Lawd, you need a good smack round yer mouth.

Dawn   Go on then. Do it. Tell me again how you wish you never had me.

Sylvia   Stop it! You think it's nonsense, fine, sweep it up, get rid of it. I have no problem with that. But don't keep expecting us to hold our hand for you.

Dawn   Well stop dumping yer shit onto us then.

Sylvia   You are putting us on a pedestal, Dawn, that we could never live up to.

Dawn   It may not be what you want but that's the way it is.

Sylvia   And now, we are all gone. Just as you will be gone, Dawn, and your sister, and your boy, one day.

Dawn   I was supposed to look out for Daryl.

Sylvia   Dawn?

Dawn   I am supposed to look after Jermaine. I know that. I accept that. But who's gonna look after me, Mum?

Sylvia   That is life child.

Dawn   Not good enough.

Sylvia   It's alright.

Dawn   So, you don't know. You have no idea!

Sylvia   It's allowed. It's allowed that you do not know.

Jermaine *comes in, as far he is concerned,* **Dawn** *is by herself, talking to herself.*

Dawn   Is that really all you have for me? For real?

Sylvia   That is all there is.

Dawn   What's dying like?

Sylvia   Not as bad as I had thought.

Dawn   You seen Daryl yet?

Sylvia   Gimme a chance nuh. You only just put me in the ground an hour ago.

Dawn   Forget I asked.

Sylvia *holds* **Dawn**'s *hand.*

Sylvia   Just, just do yer best, child.

Dawn   That's easier said.

Jermaine   Mum? What are you doing?

Dawn   You alright?

Jermaine   Am I alright? Do you want me to come back in five, so you can finish talking to yourself?

Sylvia *lets go of her daughter's hand and leaves.*

Dawn   I was just thinking about your gran.

Jermaine   Yeah, but out loud?

Dawn   You know what, Jermaine, today of all days, I don't need any one telling me what I am supposed to feel, and how I am supposed to feel it. You get?

Jermaine   OK, it just looks a bit weird, Mum, that's all.

Dawn   Why are you here?

Jermaine   I was worried about you. You dashed away from the cemetery so fast.

Dawn   Is your Aunt Marcia with you?

Jermaine   No, she wanted to take one of the cars.

Dawn   With your dad?

Jermaine   Say?

Dawn   It's not a trick question, Jermaine.

Jermaine   Yeah with him, why?

Dawn   Your Uncle Frank and his lot?

Jermaine   The next cars behind.

Dawn   They should all be here by now.

Jermaine   No, there's a big pile up on the high street now, some accident. They might have got caught in that.

Dawn   Yeah.

Jermaine   You know, if you just waited, we all could have come home together.

Dawn   I needed to be on my own.

Jermaine   To talk to yourself?

Dawn   You know, he makes me laugh, your Uncle Frank. He always knew how. I would have fallen apart if he wasn't here today, I am not lying. He's the brother I never had.

Jermaine   You had us. You still do.

Dawn   What's that, a family of liars?

Jermaine   Are you kicking off?

Dawn   I think it is safe to say that, yes.

Jermaine   Well, come on then. Bring it.

Dawn   That blasted girl, Jermaine.

Jermaine   Say her name, Mum.

Dawn   Nothing but shit white trash.

Jermaine   Don't call her that.

Dawn   What?

Jermaine   Call her anything you like, but not that. It's racist.

Dawn   Are you for real? Are you and that dutty white self seriously going to school *me* about race?

Jermaine   No.

Dawn   Heard it all now.

Jermaine   Just don't say it, Mum

Dawn   She killed your brother.

Jermaine   No, she didn't.

Dawn   I can't bring myself to look . . .

Jermaine   I love her.

Dawn   No you don't.

Jermaine   Yes I do.

Dawn   Your brother couldn't handle her, what makes you think you can?

Jermaine   Daryl never loved her, he treated her like shit.

Dawn   Watch yer mouth.

Jermaine   He did, Mum.

Dawn   That's your brother. It cannot last. It never does.

Jermaine   Stop bigging yourself up, like yer all that. You think I don't know about your whack taste in music? (*Calls.*) *Alexa*, play Dawn's kitchen playlist

Dawn   *Alexa*, stop. It's not whack.

Jermaine   Mum, it's whack.

Dawn   What do you want, all of you, what do you want me to be?

Jermaine   I don't want anything from you, listen to whatever you want.

Dawn   Did your brother hate me this much?

Jermaine   Mum?

Dawn   True talk from you.

Jermaine   He said he did, but I don't know if he ever meant it. I don't think he did, no. He did think he was better than you, better than me, better than all of us.

Dawn   Well I suppose that is something. Any parent would be mad not to want their children to be better than them. To want them to achieve something in their lives.

Jermaine   I want Simone, Mum. I'm mad for her.

Dawn   Oh, this boy!

Jermaine   What will it take?

Dawn   From her? Not a damn thing.

Jermaine   That it was my fault?

Dawn   What you say? Your fault?

Jermaine   Is that what it will take, Mum? To say that it was my fault that Daryl died? Will it? Cos I can't hold this shit in any more.

Dawn   What are you saying to me?

Jermaine   It was me that wanted to score that night, that is why we were at that club. Simone warned us, it was rough, we laughed at her. Twenty minutes later, those white boys were getting into it with Daryl, we stopped laughing. She tried to get us out safe, Mum, she really tried.

Dawn   No.

Jermaine   Yes, Mum.

Dawn   She never said.

Jermaine   Did you ever gave her a chance? You are hating her for nothing.

Dawn   May be so, but . . .

Jermaine   Maybe so what? It was my fault; did you not hear? What could you possibly have to say about her now?

Dawn   I didn't fight back then for you to be with a . . .

Jermaine   With a white woman?

Dawn (*scorns*)   Woman?

Jermaine   She dropped the charges against you, Mum. Cos she's like that, cos underneath all of her mouthy shit she's a good person. Let it go, if you want blame someone, blame me. I'm the one, I'm to blame. Not Simone. I don't mind.

Dawn   *You don't mind?*

Jermaine   I don't care.

Dawn   How long have you been storing all of that?

Jermaine   Too long. And it's like an elephant has lifted its feet off my chest.

Dawn   And those same feet are now on me. Thank you, son, thank you.

Jermaine   I aint saying all of this his to stress you out, just leave Simone out of it, yeah. Mum? Mum, you go look at me or what?

Dawn   I can't look at you, they killed your brother but *you don't mind?*

Jermaine   Like yer so better.

Dawn   You choose now to get all renk wid me?

Jermaine   What is it that you all did back then what was so special? You cuss gran about *Windrush*, how they let you down, you had to fight for your rights, you and Daryl's dad. You and my dad with your days on the front line, did you even win, if so where's the glory, Mum? Where's that perfect world for us, your kids? All you do is pick brers that you know are going to dash you one day. It's like you depend on it.

Tony *enters, followed by* **Marcia.**

Jermaine   Is this what you lot were fighting for back in the day? The right to be such shit parents now?

Dawn   So you hate me too, just like your brother?

Jermaine   I don't hate you.

Dawn   So why are you breaking my heart?

Jermaine   I'm sorry!

Tony   Hey, don't bark at yer mudda like that.

Jermaine   Perfect timing. *Brrrp!*

Tony   You have too much to say yu nuh.

Dawn   And look, it's liars number two and three.

Tony   Dawn?

Dawn   Don't come near me.

Marcia   Dawn, what is it?

Dawn   You as well, Marse.

Tony   What the hell?

Dawn   Don't come near me, or I swear, I will fling you down and smash yer face, yu nuh hear me?

Tony (*accusing* **Jermaine**)   What have you done now?

Jermaine   Nothing, man.

Tony   Don't call me *man*.

Jermaine   I just walked into this, same as you.

Dawn   My whole family, nothing but liars.

Marcia   Not today, Dawn, please?

Dawn   Yes, today.

Marcia   Do you think you are the only one who is feeling pain? She was my mother as well.

Dawn   What was that?

Marcia   What was that?

Dawn   You just took a step towards me.

Marcia   Put the bottle down.

Dawn   Do not come a step nearer.

Marcia   Lawd Jesus, Dawn.

Dawn (*raging*)   I will cut out your eye!

Marcia   Alright, I am staying here. I will not move.

Dawn   Thank you.

Tony We got have people coming, yu nuh, Dawn? They could rock up at any time, and it's now you choose to mek up noise?

Dawn Bloody all of you.

Marcia Dawn please?

Dawn You grind my sister, Tony?

Tony What?

Dawn Did you fuck her? Did you? Did you?

Tony Dawn, we need to get ourselves together, here.

Dawn Did you?

Tony This aint helping.

Dawn Did you?

Tony Come on, girl.

Jermaine Did you?

Tony Who asked you, boy?

Jermaine Answer her question then.

Tony You best tek that bass tone outta yer voice when you ask me summin.

Jermaine Like yer all that.

Tony You barking at me after all the stress you've given her?

Jermaine Who are you to come at me like you are my dad now, *Tony?*

Tony Oh I see, is that how it go?

Jermaine Dass how it go!

Dawn Still waiting, Tony.

Marcia   For what? A answer to your question that you already know? Don't make this any worse for yourself, Dawn.

Dawn   Any worse? Marcia, there is nothing left in the tank for it to be worse.

Marcia   It was back in the day. Before you and he had even met. Sit down, girl.

Jermaine   I can't deal man, I'm out of here.

Marcia   Jermaine, please.

Jermaine   I can't do this.

Tony   Hey boy, listen.

Jermaine   You've been in and out of my life like a cold, why should I listen to you now?

Dawn   Let him go.

Tony *stands out of* **Jermaine**'s *way.* **Jermaine** *leaves.*

Tony   This is just like you. Making up a whole heap of noise for yourself. So, what now, Dawn? You want me to go now, is that what this is?

Dawn   Your answer for everything Tony, is *going*.

Tony   I will go follow after Jermaine then, yeah?

Dawn   I don't give a boomba what you do!

Tony   Alright then! Everyone will be here soon. Will you please get it together?

Tony *leaves.*

Marcia   Dawn?

Dawn   Step the fuck back. Mi nuh joke.

Marcia   I'm sorry.

Dawn   Right back.

Marcia   Are you really going to hurt me if I don't?

Dawn   Like you wouldn't believe.

Marcia   I do, in fact

Dawn   Come any closer.

Marcia   I said I believe you, Dawn.

Dawn   I dare you.

Marcia   No. Not with that face.

Dawn   Good. Cos, if you had, you wouldn't believe what is happening to you, even when it's happening.

The sisters retreat to their respective corners.

Marcia   You can't stand there forever.

Dawn   Watch.

Marcia   Sooner or later, you are going to have to talk to me.

Dawn   No, I don't.

Marcia   I should have told you, a long time ago.

Dawn   Believe that.

Marcia   How the hell did you find out?

Dawn   Today, my sister. Cousin Frank. He said summin when he saw you together today. When I pressed him about it, he assumed I knew. After all of these years.

Marcia   Are you going to look at me?

Dawn   And you even had the brass neck to ask me, over and over, what I saw in him.

Marcia   It was back in the day.

Dawn   That's what makes it worse.

Marcia   Nearly forty years ago.

Dawn   Go, just leave me.

Marcia　We have guests, we have people coming,

Dawn　So let them in, just leave me alone. Can you do that?

Marcia　Right. I will leave you alone. By the way.

Dawn　Oh man!

Marcia　It's over you know.

Dawn　What is?

Marcia　My career. In case you ever find yourself wondering. Giles and I. Already I am getting *I am thinking of ending things and going back to my wife and beg forgiveness* vibe.

Dawn　You know it's almost like a work of art, how you are able to bring every conversation we have no matter the subject, back to it being about you. (*Sighs.*) Well. Come on then. Tell me what's happened now? Bring it.

Marcia　The police claim to have obtained footage from another one of their traffic cameras. According to them, this one can prove beyond a shadow, Giles was behind the wheel of the car that night. So that is it, game over, they caught me out, lying through my arse. They are coming for me.

Dawn　Girl, they were always coming for you. One way or the other.

Marcia　And you don't have a *told you* speech primed and ready for me? No, *diss is how dem white people stay* lyric?

Dawn　What can I say, you don't know already? Look, just shut up for me, Marse? One minute, yeah? What are you doing? Sit yer ass down or summin.

Marcia　No, I'll go, I'll jog on, as requested.

Dawn　I say sit.

Marcia　You're still angry, I don't blame you.

Dawn　Marse!

Marcia　OK.

Marcia *sits down.*

Dawn   There's too much going on here today, that I can't deal with. I need to bring it down; I need to bring it way down.

Marcia   Makes sense.

Dawn   Back in the day you said?

Marcia   For real.

Dawn   It happened at a *Blues* party?

Marcia   Yes, Deptford way, I think. It was such a long time ago. I was Marcia from *Craven Green* then.

Dawn   You'd fling down with anyone, you.

Marcia   Exactly. Well come, fling yerself at me.

Dawn   Don't think I wouldn't if I thought for a second it would make me feel better.

Marcia   You are too good, Dawn.

Dawn   I know that. Who else was going to look after Mum, you?

Marcia   Finally, honesty. At long last. Well, allow me to throw one back at you. Are you ready?

Dawn   Hit me.

Marcia   When I heard about Daryl, what you might be going through.

Dawn   You mean what I did go through.

Marcia   I could have been with you.

Dawn   Say?

Marcia   I said I could have been with you, Dawn. I could have got on an earlier flight. I went as far to the airport to change my flight in fact, but I didn't. I turned myself around and went back to my hotel.

Dawn   Why?

Marcia   Because I didn't want to see you like that.

Dawn   I was a mess, Marse. I was in pieces, girl.

Marcia   I know that. I know you were. I couldn't begin to imagine what state you were in, but I didn't want to see you.

Dawn   Why didn't you want to see me?

Marcia   I didn't want the drama. I didn't want to think about it. I didn't want to be alone with you. I knew I couldn't handle it. I'm sorry.

Dawn   But you were at the funeral.

Marcia   Did you not notice, that I was never alone with you, not in a single room? I couldn't handle it.

Dawn   You're my sister.

Marcia   You are nothing but trauma, Dawn, you always have been. And I have always have been a selfish bitch, you know that. You've said that.

Dawn   Even Mum was there for me. Even Tony.

Marcia   I couldn't handle it, Dawn, I couldn't handle you anymore, what do you want?

Dawn   Well, that's fucked.

Marcia   See it deh. The defence rests.

Dawn   I bet it does.

Marcia   Come at me if you like. Lay it on. What are you waiting?

Dawn   No.

Marcia   No?

Dawn   You deaf? I said no.

Marcia   What's the matter with you?

Dawn Not a thing, but I think I understand.

Marcia You think?

Dawn Yes Marse, *I think*. It's been known to happen. If I couldn't handle myself, what chance could you have?

Marcia Where'd you get off being so damned nice?

Dawn You call this nice?

Marcia I said I wasn't there for you, Dawn.

Dawn OK then, would you like your arse beaten, here and now?

Marcia Yes, come on, get it out of the way.

Dawn Why do you want me to hurt you?

Marcia I deserve it.

Dawn No you don't.

Marcia I deserve it all. To uppity, too ambitious for my own good, yes? White must be right, I find out now though, innit? I find out good.

Dawn Marse.

Marcia I didn't know my place, that was my problem. Nothing but a damn coconut. A bounty bar.

Dawn Hey, enough of that!

Marcia Giles got a taste of ebony. For years, I rolled over for him like a dog as he came back for more. From the time that I was nine, I told myself I was better than you. I sexed yer man in someone's bathroom. I weren't there for you when your boy died. Come on girl, lay me out.

Dawn Sit down.

Marcia I beg you, Dawn, please, stop don't being so damn kind to me.

Dawn Yu nuh hear me say, sit?

Tony *hovers by the door. They do not see him at first.*

Dawn   Is beating you up going to bring Daryl back to me? Is it going to get your life back? Make me forgive, Jermaine?

Marcia   Jermaine?

Dawn   Tell me that it will, tell me everything that is going on inside my head can go, right now, and I will beat your arse like a drum if that is what it cost.

Tony (*goes to the front door*)   Can you two not hear the door?

Marcia   I'm so sorry.

Dawn   You said that. I got that. Can we just park that now? You're still my sister, yer mad arse bitch, and I need you.

Marcia *and* **Dawn** *see* **Tony** *who has let in* **PC Spencer**.

Tony   I think it's for you, Marse.

Marcia   Funny.

Tony *goes upstairs.*

Dawn   Well hello there. PC Ayesha Spencer. Are you for real? Today of all days?

PC Spencer   I'm sorry about this.

Dawn   You made it through the traffic I see. The boys at your nick must have a hard on this big to want to arrest my sister.

Marcia   Dawn?

Dawn   Well, come on then, come nuh, do what you have to do, make your family proud.

PC Spencer (*formal*)   Marcia Adams, I am arresting you . . .

Marcia   Please don't, let's just go. Shall we?

PC Spencer   You don't remember me, do you?

Marcia   Should I?

PC Spencer   Four years ago, you were the defence lawyer on a case I was giving evidence in. Attempted murder. You cross examined me; you gave me a really hard time.

Marcia   I wondered what that cold air from you was about.

PC Spencer   It was my first time in court. You tore me to shreds.

Marcia   Was I supposed to feel sorry for you?

PC Spencer   I was a little unprepared. I was nervous.

Marcia   Next time, don't be.

PC Spencer   You made me look like I was falsifying evidence.

Marcia   Were you?

PC Spencer   You ought to know about that.

Dawn   Oh yes, she's a Spencer. Watch her face.

PC Spencer   I suppose one only needs to have a double-barrelled name to obtain the services of the great Marcia Adams QC.

Marcia   What is your point, Constable?

PC Spencer   The man I was giving evidence against, Lord Money Bags or whatever his name is, was acquitted.

Marcia   I'm sorry.

PC Spencer   You're sorry? He went back to the house that very day and finished what he had started. He beat his wife to a pulp. She died on her way to hospital. You should be sorry.

Marcia   No, no, what I meant was, I'm sorry you weren't able to get your shit together.

PC Spencer   What?

Marcia   Build a better case.

Dawn   Boom! See it deh!

PC Spencer   My colleagues blamed me. They said I was too inexperienced. Too female. Too black.

Marcia   Like I say, shit. Together.

PC Spencer   Right. I see.

Marcia   Did you always want to join the police, Constable Spencer?

PC Spencer   Look, if you are about to give me the *work twice as hard to prove we are as good* speech, I have heard it.

Marcia   The law has been my life for over thirty years but even now, black barristers make up just over one per cent of QCs at the bar. I have lost count the amount of times I have been mistaken for a defendant. Do you know what I do, Constable? Before anyone can make an assumption, I try to say something like *I'm a barrister* or *I am looking for my client* or *I need a room to prepare my witness, I've got a case today in court number 12, Let me through.* I drop them as early as I can into the conversation. It is all about belief as well as confidence. I don't give any of them the opportunity to question my status. Do not apologise for what you are, Constable Spencer. Do not give them the satisfaction. Do not give them the opportunity to question your status. Do what you can to turn that corner.

PC Spencer   You sound just like my mum.

Marcia   Do what you can to turn that corner.

Dawn   Except that is shit, Marse.

Marcia   Shall we?

Dawn   No, hold up a sec. That is shit, girl, you know it is. Turn that corner? I mean cha rass!

Dawn *slams the bottle down on the coffee table.*

Marcia   OK, we really need to go. My sister is now on *Wray and Nephew* time.

Dawn   We do nothing but turn corners, and what do we find, another corner? We turn again, another corner. We go around and around, and around, and around, turning nothing but mother fucking corners.

Marcia   Please excuse her.

Dawn   Don't apologise for me.

Marcia   It was our mother's funeral today. She's still upset. She needs time.

Dawn   They are the ones who seem to need the bloody time, Marse. All of the time in the whole bloody world it would seem. How much more time do you think they want, Constable Spencer?

PC Spencer   Calm down, Ms Adams.

Dawn   What do you mean, calm down? Have you not been listening? Have you not been witnessing your entire life? Have a word with your black self, man.

Marcia   Dawn?

Dawn   White people, dem so! How much more time do you think they want? From us?

PC Spencer   Move away, please?

Dawn   You don't have nuttin, not an idea?

PC Spencer   Right now.

Dawn   Your time? Your family's time? My time? My sister's time? My cousin's time? My boyfriend's time? My mum and dad's time? My son's time? I mean how much more time? Marse?

Marcia   Dawn, please?

Dawn   That fucking Giles.

Marcia   Don't.

Dawn   I go kill him.

PC Spencer   Excuse me?

Dawn   Spineless good for nothing bumbo, rassclaart.

Marcia   Dawn, stop it.

PC Spencer   I don't know what this is, Miss Adams.

Dawn   Don't try and school me, girl.

PC Spencer   But I would advise you, most strongly, to listen to your sister.

Dawn   So advise, come bring it.

Marcia   Lawd Jesus, Dawn.

Dawn   Thirty years of your life, Marse.

Marcia   Shut up.

Dawn   Everything you have worked for.

Marcia   Do you think I do not know this?

Dawn   They can't ask you to do it.

Marcia (*snaps*)   But they are not asking me!

Dawn   So that's it?

Marcia   Don't make this worse.

Dawn   Them white people win again. Mum and Dad, you and me, Daryl and Jermaine, they do it to us again, and again and again.

Marcia (*to* **Spencer**)   Have you heard enough now?

PC Spencer   Miss Adams!

Dawn   Come on, Marse?

Marcia   Dawn, don't mek me slap you.

Dawn   Mi want fire bun every last stinking one a' dem!

Marcia   Stop it. Stop it. Stop it.

Tony *returns from upstairs.*

Marcia *gently holds* **Dawn**'s *face in her hands.*

Marcia   I got this. I'll be alright. It'll be alright.

Marcia *gently kisses her sister on the forehead in order to calm her down.*

Marcia (*to* **Spencer**)   Please?

Marcia *and* **Spencer** *leave together.*

Tony   Hate to say, but what goes around.

Dawn   Then don't say it.

Tony   What?

Dawn   If you hate to say it, then don't say it. Don't say anything.

Tony   OK.

Dawn   *OK?*

Tony   Frank texted. The traffic's cleared up, everyone will be here in about ten.

Dawn   OK, Tony?

Tony   Shall I leave it to you to tell them about Marcia?

Dawn   What do you by mean *OK?*

Tony   I mean, OK.

Dawn   Is that it?

Tony   What else is there?

Dawn   Don't you ever get tired of it all?

Tony   Tired of what?

Dawn　The fight, Tony. Us versus them. White against black.

Tony　You didn't sound tired a second ago.

Dawn　Just answer the question.

Tony　No.

Dawn　Not even sometimes?

Tony　We can't afford to, Dawn.

Dawn　When was the last time you have been on a march, Tony? When was the last time there has ever been a march? A real fight about something, anything, that's made the slightest difference for us? Why don't you ever call me *babe*?

Tony　What?

Dawn　Tell me that I'm buff?

Tony　*Buff?*

Dawn　For once, just once, man.

Tony　Dawn . . . what?

Dawn　Oh, nuh mind.

Tony　You want me to call you *babe* now?

Dawn　Just forget it.

Tony　I'm sorry.

Dawn　Yer sorry?

Tony　Yes!

Dawn　For what?

Tony　For whatever it is that you have the arsehole about now.

Dawn　You know what man, fuck off.

Tony　Dawn?

Dawn   Fuck off mi say.

Tony   Fine then, I'll get my things.

Dawn   Yes, that's your answer.

Tony   That's what you want.

Dawn   You can't even wait to leave.

Tony   You just tell me to tek my arse out, make up yer mind, woman. What you chat 'bout? What do you want, Dawn?

Dawn   Don't you know, don't you know anything about me?

Tony   *Babe?*

Dawn   Don't!

Tony   Oh, you are giving me a headache here.

Dawn   You have got it so easy haven't you, Tony?

Tony   You call any of this easy?

Dawn   My mum was buried today. I saw her lowered into the earth. I had one great aunt to my right, some distant cousin to my left, both of them, out of tune I might add, bellowing, screeching even, for the whole of south to hear, *How great thou art*. And where were you? Half a mile away.

Tony   What are you talking about, I was there.

Dawn   Standing under a bloody tree you were. Smoking a cigar. Not a cigarette. A cigar, Tony. I saw you. Who does that?

Tony   I like cigars.

Dawn   When you should have been with me, holding my hand, having some idea how I am feeling.

Tony   I was there. Jermaine was there. Marse was there.

Dawn   On my own, Tony.

Tony   Come on.

Dawn   On my own, on my own, inside.

Tony   Oh cha!

Dawn   Wondering why you can't bring your arse over here to me, so I can cling to you, feel you, know that you care.

Tony   I do care.

Dawn   You care about your band; you care about your gigs, your music, your bloody saxophone. I just don't believe you care about me.

Tony   I care that you are crying on right now, like some blasted white woman. You don't feel shame?

Dawn   So, the hell what?

Tony   Why don't you call yourself *Karen* and be done with it.

Dawn   Trust me, I'd be the most annoying frigid privileged whitest insecure *Karen* woman there is, if it meant I don't feel what am I feeling right now. I like privilege Tony. I want some privilege in my life. Just a lickle piece, how can that be too much to ask?

Tony   You carry on like I lied to you. I never lied to you, Dawn. I have told you nuff times, I don't do nine-to-five, I'm not built that way. I don't do that.

Dawn   Flinging down women is what you do, my own sister.

Tony   Here it come again.

Dawn   I wanna rip yer wurtless spine out.

Tony   Thirty-five years ago, some rhatid blues party, in the bathroom of someone's house, I can't even remember. I didn't even know you.

Dawn   I don't business, I still want to kill you.

Tony   Frank tell you, innit? Him open his mout!

Dawn   You mek me sick.

Tony   Yes, Dawn, I think I've got that, as well as the whole of south. So, what now?

Dawn   When you're here, you are always letting me down, I am never in your heart, I am tired of it.

Tony   What do want, Dawn?

Dawn   Share with me.

Tony   Share what?

Dawn   Everything. Talk with me. Yell with me, cry with me, make love with me, dance with me, yes, yes, yes, dance with me, right now, dance with me to this. Come on. (*Calls.*) *Alexa*, play my kitchen playlist.

Music plays.

Tony   Are you having a laugh?

Dawn   Nope.

Tony   You like this?

Dawn   I love this! (*Sings along.*) Come on!

Tony   Another thing you kept quiet.

Dawn   I have a whole heap of stuff I've kept quiet about, you want to hear?

Tony   Not really.

Dawn   I had my first orgasm over a poster of *John Travolta*. I agree with every word *Piers Morgan* says about *Meghan Markle*. I think *Arsenal* are shit. I read *The Daily Mail*. I think *Phil Mitchell* is a sex god. I believe *La La Land* should have won the *Oscar*. I want to execute the next black person that goes on *MasterChef* and cooks jerk chicken. I find the work of *Maya Angelou* so bloody boring. I wish black boys would stop wearing hoodies. I wish black girls would learn to say *please as well as thank you!* I am embarrassed on a daily basis, that you play sax in a UB40 tribute band. I don't want *Idris Elba* to play *James Bond*. *Everybody's Talking about Jamie* is the greatest musical ever. *Hamilton* is self-indulgent sexist crap. *Spike Lee* is overrated. *Viola Davis* is no *Meryl Streep*. And I live as well as die for *Strictly*!

Tony   Are you done?

Dawn   Just dance, man.

Tony   People are coming, Dawn.

Dawn   Let them come. Let them watch. (*Pleads.*) Dance with me, dance with the woman you say you love.

Tony   But this is shit.

Dawn   I know it's shit. It's white man formulaic, bland as it can be, naff as you like, centuries old, low-down, pale skin, shit. But I want to dance to it, and I want you to dance with me. I won't tell your brers, dance with me. (*Waits.*) What is the matter with you?

Tony *has no idea where to put himself.*

Dawn   *Alexa*, pause.

The music pauses.

Tony   I'm sorry, yeah. I can't.

Dawn   Stop talking, Tony. Just close your mouth for me. Leave now. And don't ever come back.

Tony   Come on, girl . . .

Dawn   Who are you calling, *girl?*

Tony   Dawn, let's just . . .

Dawn   Do you not understand me, Tony? Did you not hear? I want your wurtless black arse self to leave. Don't mek me holler, yeah?

Tony   Holler? What you think I'm ging to do . . . I ain't like that.

Dawn   You ain't nuttin. Leave mi say.

Tony Whose hollering now?

Dawn Just leave, Tony. Now.

Tony *leaves.*

Dawn *Alexa*, play *Madonna.*

Music plays.

Dawn *continues to sing along as well as dance alone.*

Scene Four

A few hours later.

Tony *is packing his bag furiously with his clothes. He finds more of his clothes in the tumble dryer.*

Jermaine *arrives through the front door.*

Tony So, it's now you reach.

Jermaine Now you preach?

Tony I'm just trying to have a conversation, my yout.

Jermaine That's all you do man, you try.

Tony It's one in the morning.

Jermaine And now I want my bed.

Tony You saw her tonight?

Jermaine Saw who?

Tony Come on. You know.

Jermaine What if?

Tony I'd take that as a yes.

Jermaine Take it how you like.

Tony She knows you told your mum the truth?

Jermaine What did you say?

Tony   About Daryl?

Jermaine   How do you know about that?

Tony   Cos I know your brother was no saint. Cos I know how he felt about you and your mum. Cos I know it was you that wanted a score that night. Cos I'm not as *wurtless* or as stupid or as blind as you all think.

Jermaine   Yet here you are, packing your shit, again.

Tony   Yes, mi dat, see it deh.

Jermaine   Alright then, Tony, see you next year, maybe.

Tony   Believe dat!

Jermaine   I do believe *dat*. Mind yourself.

Tony   Meaning?

Jermaine   There's some of sort of mad bug out there, they say it's as easy as catching the cold, but twice as deadly, is what I mean. Have you had your flu jab?

Tony   You chat like I'm old.

Jermaine   You are old.

Tony   Maybe. But I'm proud of you.

Jermaine   Proud? You want to end it with that?

Tony   So, what you want?

Jermaine   From you? (*Laughs.*)

Tony   Yeah, laugh it off, my yout.

Jermaine   I intend.

Tony   You should have come to me.

Jermaine   Of course.

Tony   Not that I go along with any of that shit, cos I don't, I never have, but still if you wanted a score or summin, you should have come to me.

Jermaine   Why does everyone have to come to you? Why can't you crawl your arse over to me for once?

Time for you to hit the road, man, so go if you're going.

Tony   You know, I would have like my dad to say he was proud of me.

Jermaine (*cringes*)   Oh my!

Tony   To feel that, you know. From him. I would have liked that a lot. But he was always too busy planning another demo. Brixton here, New Cross there, making no end of noise on the front line.

Jermaine   Musta been when he wasn't having a squeeze of Mum's arse when you weren't looking, yeah? Any woman's arse come to that. Mum told me.

Tony   I bet she did. I still would have liked it.

Jermaine   If that's how you feel.

Tony (*pleads*)   Jermaine?

Jermaine   No, no more, I want my bed.

Tony   Wait a second.

Jermaine   For what, man?

Tony   If she's the one, Simone.

Jermaine   Don't say it.

Tony   The only one.

Jermaine   Tony, for real?

Tony   Don't let her go, boy.

Jermaine   Did you not hear, don't say that to me. Simone and I are good.

Tony   Am glad to hear.

Jermaine   We will work to make it work; you get? You, Mum, Auntie Marse, need to take a seat man cos yer done. Yer old.

Tony   Easy to say . . .

Jermaine   . . . my yout? Why don't you try for me? All of yer, just try.

Tony   You say there's a mad bug going round?

Jermaine   I'm not saying it, the news are saying it.

Tony   I best go see a doctor then, get my flu jab, take a seat, seeing as I am done, as well as old!

Jermaine   Might be best.

Tony   Your mudda needs you.

Jermaine   I know that.

Tony   Big time.

Jermaine   I said I know.

Tony   I'll keep in touch, yeah.

Jermaine   No, you won't.

Tony   You keep swinging, little man.

Tony *grabs his saxophone. He goes.*

Scene Five

A month later.

Marcia *is taking the stand.*

Marcia   On the evening of Monday October eighteenth of this year, I was a passenger in the car driven by Mister Giles Mortimer. By the time I had stepped into the vehicle, Mister Mortimer was already intoxicated. I had asked him several times to allow me to drive, which he refused. Nevertheless,

I remained in the passenger side as I feared he may harm himself or others. During the course of the journey, I had warned Mister Mortimer several times to slow down, as he was speeding as well as driving erratically. Mister Mortimer had dismissed my concerns. The following day, due to his several other speeding offences in the past, his concern that he may have his driving licence suspended, and that his political career was under threat, Mister Mortimer had asked me to inform the police that I was the one driving the car on the night of October eighteenth, I had agreed to do so. That was a lie and I was fully aware of the consequences of making a false statement, which I did so anyway, due to my personal as well as intimate relationship with Mister Giles Mortimer. I would like to sincerely apologise to the police and to this court for my part in this very serious case of criminal deceit.

Scene Six

Later that day.

The living room.

Dawn   I would have loved to have seen that *renk's* face in that court room. I would have paid money.

Marcia   I did.

Dawn   Him face favour batty now!

Marcia   I almost felt sorry for him.

Dawn   Sorry?

Marcia   I said almost.

Dawn   The brer's a chief.

Marcia   *Brer?*

Dawn   And she's off.

Marcia   *Chief?*

Dawn   Yeah, I know I know, leave that for the *Jermaine* and *Simone's* of the world.

Message received.

Marcia   You said her name. *Simone.*

Dawn   I know what I said.

Marcia   How does that feel?

Dawn   That I'm working on it.

Marcia   You are doing good.

Dawn   Don't praise me. I cannot lose another one, Marse. My heart won't take it. Besides, once he finds out she can't cook as well as me, and she learns he doesn't like his hair been touched, I'll give it six months.

Marcia   Or maybe they will go the distance.

Dawn   Or maybe you'll get a slap so hard with one of my tits.

Marcia   You call dem sags, tits?

Dawn   Are you calling me fat?

Marcia   Well when did you last eat a salad?

Dawn   I want what he wants. That is all I can do for him.

Marcia   Listen to us.

Dawn   *Innit!*

Marcia   No doubt now, sis. We're the old farts. Cheers.

Dawn   Salut!

They clink their glasses.

Dawn   So, what now for you?

Marcia   Dawn, please just let me drink.

Dawn   Tell me.

Marcia   I shall be disbarred. A custodial sentence is possible. (*Before* **Dawn** *can say anything.*) No, don't call, don't cry, don't scream. Don't do anything. I beg.

Dawn   I wasn't going to say anything.

Marcia   Lie bad.

Dawn   But that is fucked.

Marcia   See you!

Dawn   But it is though.

Marcia   It is what it is, Dawn.

Dawn   Is it?

Marcia   Why do you love to go on so?

Dawn   Is it Marse? Is any of this fair?

Marcia (*about to crack*)   No. You want to hear me say it out loud, no it is not fair.

Dawn   So what is it then?

Marcia   Jesus, Dawn. What are you doing to me?

Dawn   Talk to me, sis.

Marcia   I engaged in conduct which was dishonest and discreditable. I engaged in conduct which was prejudicial to the administration of justice as well as likely to diminish public confidence in the legal profession. What part of any of that do you not get?

Dawn *can see* **Marcia** *is breaking into tears.*

Dawn   Over here. Come now.

Marcia *rushes into her sisters arms, before bursting into floods of tears.*

Marcia   I loved him.

Dawn   I know you did.

Marcia   Don't you laugh at me.

Dawn   I'm not laughing.

Marcia   I'm scared, sis.

*It is **Dawn**'s turn to hold her sister's face in her hands.*

Dawn   You see my face? Do you see anything other than some crazy arse little sister who loves her crazy arse big sister more than any crazy arse little sister could ever love anything else in the world? All that love for a big sister who made an art form of pissing off our mudda, just so she would go for her with her belt instead of me? Do you see her, Marse?

Dawn *plants a kiss on her forehead.*

Dawn   This is the hard time. So, suck it up. And with that in mind, there is only one thing left for us to do. You get?

Marcia (*sighs*)   Seriously?

Dawn   Come, fix yourself.

Marcia   They'll both be here in a sec.

Dawn   We're doing this. You call it.

Marcia (*calls*)   *Alexa*, play *Wham*.

Music plays.

Dawn   Yes, George.

Marcia   Gwan, Andrew!

Dawn   Make it right for us.

Together, the sisters dance.

*It goes a on for a good minute until **Jermaine**, followed by **Simone** walk in. They look astonished.*

Marcia *is first to see them. She indicates to **Dawn**.*

Dawn   *Alexa*, pause.

The music stops.

Dawn What's up boy, you're never seen your mudda dance before?

Jermaine I know we're early. We could come back.

Dawn Bring yourselves in, come on.

Jermaine *and* **Simone** *step in to the room.*

Jermaine This is my Aunt Marcia.

Marcia Hey girl.

Simone (*a little nervous*) Hello.

Marcia Good to meet you at last.

Jermaine No *Kylie Minogue* today, Mum?

Dawn I'm happy to surprise you.

Jermaine I don't even know what one that was.

Simone It's *Wham,* babe.

Jermaine Say what?

Simone *George Michael? Andrew Ridgeley?*

Dawn You like *Wham,* Simone?

Simone One of my mum's favourites. Still are.

Dawn Oh yes?

Simone Every time it's on, she'd make us all dance with her in the living room.

Dawn Is that right, Simone? Is that so?

Simone Yeah . . . (*Realises.*) Hold up, Oh no, no, no.

Dawn What you afraid of?

Simone Nothing.

Dawn Well then?

Simone Yeah but . . .

Dawn   What?

Simone   Come on.

Dawn   You brought it up.

Simone   Yeah, I did, didn't I?

Dawn   Come show us. Bring some moves.

Jermaine   Mum, you cannot make her dance if she don't want to.

Dawn   Who said anything about just her?

Jermaine   What?

Dawn   You used to love a bit of *Wham* when you was little.

Simone   Oh yes?

Dawn   You and your little fat legs couldn't get enough of *Georgie*.

Jermaine   Yeah alright, can we just park that, please?

Simone   If I do it, you do it.

Dawn   Bring yourself the two a yer. *Alexa* resume!

Music plays.

Jermaine   Auntie, you go help me out here?

Marcia   Don't look at me, the case is hereby dismissed.

Jermaine   Only judges say that.

Marcia   Not today.

Jermaine   Mum, what you doing?

Dawn   Am trying. That OK with you?

Jermaine (*grateful*)   Alright.

Simone (*teasing*)   You and yer little fat legs, eh?

Jermaine   Jam yer hype, man. I cannot believe this.

Simone *rubs* **Jermaine**'s *hair teasingly. He giggles.* **Marcia** *gasps. She points this out to* **Dawn**.

Dawn   Not. One. Word. (*Calls.*) Come, we go do this or not?

Together, they all dance.

End.